GREEN BAY
BEER

GREEN BAY
BEER

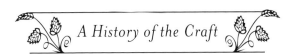

A History of the Craft

CAMERON TESKE

AMERICAN PALATE

Published by American Palate
A Division of The History Press
Charleston, SC
www.historypress.com

Cover: Courtesy of Jason Manders, Core Crafted Designs & Trail Genius.

First published 2020

Manufactured in the United States

ISBN 9781467140775

Library of Congress Control Number: 2020934325

Notice: The information in this book is true and complete to the best of our knowledge. It is offered without guarantee on the part of the author or The History Press. The author and The History Press disclaim all liability in connection with the use of this book.

To those who brew, pour, serve, drink and enjoy quality beer in Green Bay.

Cheers!

CONTENTS

CONTENTS

FOREWORD

I met Cameron during the summer of 2018, when he first came to the Local History and Genealogy Department of the Brown County Library. He was researching the breweries of Green Bay's past and heard that I shared a similar interest. Over the next year and a half, I encouraged Cameron with his research, offering tidbits of information that I found while reading the old newspapers or when I stumbled on images of the breweries.

Cameron traces Green Bay's love for beer from the first brewery in the area to our growing craft beer industry. His work examines the establishment of the brewery industry using newspaper accounts, stories and public records of the area. *Green Bay Beer: A History of the Craft* is more than just facts and dates about a building—it traces the struggles and achievements of the people who worked in the brewing industry. He shows that the tradition and knowledge of brewing beer was an occupation handed down from generation to generation in one's family.

He also looks at the struggles of the industry as competition increased from larger brewing companies. And we cannot forget the biggest struggle of all: Prohibition—the noble experiment to better our country from the evils of alcohol. Cameron explains how our local breweries tried to survive during those thirteen years, with two breweries continuing and one never reopening.

Cameron not only follows the early breweries of Green Bay but also looks at the current establishments in the area. He shows how beer making may have been dormant for thirty years, but today, it has made a strong comeback in Green Bay. With the new brewers, Cameron relays how a hobby has grown into a small craft brewing industry. And the new beers are not about tradition as much as experimenting and developing new beers for a new generation of beer drinkers. It is more about an experience than a beverage.

May this book be more than a history of Green Bay's breweries but a source of pride for the families who were once involved in brewing and those who will carry on the tradition for years to come.

—Dennis R. Jacobs
Library Associate
Local History and Genealogy Department
Brown County Library

PREFACE

What are the first three words that pop into your head when you hear someone mention Wisconsin? Beer, brats and cheese probably. If you're thinking Green Bay specifically, the Packers will most likely make the list as well. The very first word, though, is beer. Wisconsin has a rich beer history full of tradition. A Thrillist article published in early 2016 named Green Bay an "untapped beer city poised to blow up." The writer must have missed the Green Bay brewing section in history class. Green Bay's beer has been tapped for more than a century and a half. If you, too, skipped this section in your history class, pour your favorite Green Bay brew and read on to learn about this popular but lesser-known part of local history.

ACKNOWLEDGEMENTS

I had no idea how many people it would take to write a book, but I've been overwhelmed with the helpfulness and support from so many. I couldn't be more thankful for everyone who helped make this book a reality. I will do my best to not leave anyone off this list. If, on the off chance, I do, please get in touch with me. Don't yell at me too much, and I'll take you out for a beer to buy your forgiveness and drink for your friendship again.

I first need to thank my late wife, Lauren. While she and I were sitting around the firepit in our backyard on my twenty-eighth birthday, most likely drinking a local Green Bay beer, she asked me what I wanted to do with the fresh year ahead of me. My response was something along the lines of wanting to write a book before I turned thirty. No matter how sick she got, she encouraged and pushed me to follow through with this dream. I submitted this book a few weeks before that thirtieth birthday. It's devastating that she isn't here to read it.

The next person I need to thank is John Rodrigue, commissioning editor at The History Press and Arcadia Publishing. He probably has no idea how superb his timing was. John first reached out to me with a chance to write a book less than six weeks after that conversation around the firepit in my backyard. Thank you, John, for this opportunity. And thank you for your continued patience throughout the process.

A special thank you to my family: Mom and Dad, for always being supportive, for teaching me that I can do anything I work hard at and for probably being the first ones to buy my first book; my brother, Evan, for always providing a good laugh, always being up for a beer and helping with other things so that I could focus on writing.

Thank you to my son, Brekken, for already loving to read, often many books every night, even if it is to delay the inevitable bedtime. Sometimes I'm a sucker and fall for it; I'm sorry for the times I'm not.

Thank you to the people who helped with research: Deb Anderson at University of Wisconsin–Green Bay Archives; Kevin Cullen from Neville Public Museum; Dennis Jacobs and Mary Jane Herber at Brown County Library and Brown County Historical Society; Chuck Golueke from Brown County Historical Society; Jerry Strebel, a local beer memorabilia collector; and John Parsons, owner of House of Homebrew and president of Green Bay Rackers Homebrew Club.

Thank you to Brad Toll and the Greater Green Bay Convention and Visitors Bureau for giving me an opportunity to learn and love Green Bay, especially its breweries.

Thank you to all of the folks from the current breweries, who spent plenty of time with me to help tell their stories: Brent Weycker from Titletown Brewing Company; Bill Tressler from Hinterland Brewing Company; Brad Stillmank from Stillmank Brewing Company; Andrew Fabry from Badger State Brewing Company; Melissa "Missy" Martens from Copper State Brewing Company; and Marv, Alex and Tyler Falish from Noble Roots Brewing Company.

Thank you to two other local history authors who shared advice and warnings on writing a research book: David Siegel, author of *Forces of Change*, and Tim Freiss, who wrote *Haunted Green Bay*.

There were many friends who continually showed interest in the project and provided encouragement throughout the process. There were even more friends who happily drank beer with me as a much-needed distraction throughout the past couple years. Thank you to each and every one of you for so many things!

Thank you to all of you showing an interest in history and beer by reading this book. History and beer are even better when you combine them.

Thank you to everyone who continues to drink local beer. Your brewers very much appreciate it.

INTRODUCTION

Green Bay traces its recordable European roots to 1634, when French explorer Jean Nicolet arrived on the shore where the Bay of Green Bay meets the mouth of the Fox River. Nicolet was greeted by the Ho-Chunk Native people. This was the first documented contact between a European and a Native American in what would eventually become the state of Wisconsin.

French fur traders and missionaries soon followed. The French called this place *La Baye*. They used this location as a major entry point into the middle of the new continent. The French remained in control until the British overthrew them in 1763, as part of a global conflict called the Seven Years' War but known in America as the French and Indian War. The British had a short reign in the area as the American Revolution came, conquered and went.

The Americans then built Fort Howard at the turn of the nineteenth century to protect the entrance to the rest of the state of Wisconsin by way of the Bay of Green Bay. The fort brought rapid growth. Belgian farmers and Norwegian skilled workers began moving to the area in the mid-1800s. Most immigrants to Wisconsin, however, were German. Between 1820 and 1860, more than seven million people from the German states found their way to America, drawn by the dual attractions of available land and religious freedom and often pushed from their native lands during the many political upheavals of the mid-nineteenth century. By 1860, nearly a quarter of Wisconsin's residents were born in Germany. This German population brought their religions and industries. Their most well-known, and well-loved, industry was, of course, brewing beer.

Other major industries focused on iron smelting, lumber milling and paper products. This community, and its companies, has had a global impact on the paper industry ever since the mid-nineteenth century. Green Bay was also home to the first newspaper in Wisconsin.

Lumber mills began popping up in many ports along the Bay of Green Bay. Lumberjacking was a popular job in the winter for farm boys who were looking to make some extra money during the slow season. Logging was a winter job. These lumberjacks earned a rowdy reputation. They would head into town after long stints in the isolated Northwoods and wreak havoc during a night out.

There was rapid growth of breweries opening across the entire state of Wisconsin as these German immigrants came to the States. The availability of barley and hops was a huge advantage, as was the ease of access to fresh water. Green Bay's Fox River ran right through the middle of town. According to *Headlight*, a publication promoting destinations on the Chicago & Northwest Railroad, at the time, "Green Bay beer [was] noted for its fine flavor, rich and nutritious quality, and [was] pronounced by connoisseurs 'a perfect beer.' It may be stated with absolute truth that the finest brew of the celebrated Milwaukee breweries [was] not superior to that produced in Green Bay."

At first, alcohol was a point of contention between these new European immigrants and those who had been born in America. The native born were shocked at the drinking habits of the Germans. The biggest issue was the practice of "continental Sunday," in which German families gathered in the local beer hall following church.

In 1870, all five of the original Green Bay breweries were open at the same time—Blesch Brewing, Hochgreve Brewing, Rahr Brewing, Hagemeister Brewing and Van Dycke Brewing.

Life on the brewery front was going well in Green Bay until 1919 rolled around. As the Green Bay Packers were forming as a professional football team, things seemed like they couldn't get any better. That assumption was exactly true; things were about to get much worse.

One year later, Prohibition banned the production, importation, transportation and sale of alcoholic beverages. This left 2.9 million thirsty people around the state of Wisconsin. But Prohibition didn't stop them from getting what they wanted. In a Prohibition survey of Wisconsin, the federal government determined Wisconsin to be one of the wettest states, "where everybody drinks their fill and John Barleycorn still holds forth in splendor." John Barleycorn was a popular euphemism for alcohol. Some of the breweries in Green Bay survived this downtime, while others did not.

Following the repeal of Prohibition, brewing and Green Bay limped along, a sad shadow of its former self. But that by no means meant the people of the city had lost their thirst. A *Green Bay Press-Gazette* front-page story from November 1969 shared research that titled Green Bay as the beer drinking capital of the United States. Without question, more beer, the report stated, was consumed in Green Bay than anywhere else in the country. The amount of beer consumed here was 133 percent more than the national average, and yet Green Bay didn't even have any of its own breweries.

That changed over time. There are many breweries thriving in Green Bay once again. Whether the city consumes more beer than any place in the United States remains to be seen. But one thing cannot be denied or doubted: local beer is back in Green Bay in a big way. And it's never tasted better.

Part I.

BEER: A HISTORY

Beer is proof that God loves us and wants us to be happy.
—Benjamin Franklin, misquoted

Water. Grain. Hops. Yeast. The four simple ingredients responsible for making beer. How each one is used is determined by the artistic and scientific mind of the brewer. Fritz Maytag, father of modern-day microbreweries, is *correctly* quoted as saying, "We brewers don't make beer, we just get all the ingredients together and the beer makes itself… beer does not make itself properly by itself. It takes an element of mystery and of things that no one can understand." As a pioneer in microbrewing, he may have imbibed a bit of his own brew before spewing that quote. Regardless, there is much truth to this enigma of a statement. Beer is made from chemical reactions as starch is broken down to sugars and fermented by yeast to produce alcohol. The flavors of the beer, well, that's up to the brewer. And what a wonderful and infinite variety the capable brewer has at his or her beck and call—ale yeast or lager yeast (and which strain of either, or even a hybrid yeast); the color of the malt, how much and in what proportions to use them; what kind or kinds of hops to throw into the mix and when and how much; whether to add adjuncts like rice or corn; and what kind of water to tie it all together. These and a multiplicity of other decisions are made with care and regard by your friendly neighborhood brewer. May you enjoy the product of their sweat and toil. (Though, hopefully, without any sweat in the beer.)

Beer has a long history. Evidence of barley beer residue was first discovered in an archaeological dig in what is now known as Iran. It is estimated to be from about 3,000 BC. Many believe beer is much older than that, though. While an official beer invention date has long been debated, it is well known that ancient people thoroughly enjoyed beer. Babylonians had nearly twenty recipes for a variety of beer. Egyptian pharaohs oversaw brewing schedules, making them some of the earliest brewmasters. The workers who spent hot days building the pyramids were given beer as part of their compensation for construction. It might be safe to ascertain that beer helped build one of the Seven Wonders of the World.

The first official written beer recipe was found in a poem dating to almost four millennia ago. The poem, "Hymn to Ninkasi," was etched into a clay tablet found in modern-day Iraq:

Borne of the flowing water,
Tenderly cared for by the Ninhursag,
Borne of the flowing water,
Tenderly cared for by the Ninhursag,

Having founded your town by the sacred lake,
She finished its great walls for you,
Ninkasi, having founded your town by the sacred lake,
She finished its walls for you,

Your father is Enki, Lord Nidimmud,
Your mother is Ninti, the queen of the sacred lake.
Ninkasi, your father is Enki, Lord Nidimmud,
Your mother is Ninti, the queen of the sacred lake.

You are the one who handles the dough [and] did you with a big shovel,
Mixing in a pit, the bappir with sweet aromatics,
Ninkasi, you are the one who handles the dough [and] with a big shovel,
Mixing in a pit, the bappir with [date]—honey,

You are the one who bakes the bappir in the big oven,
Puts in order the piles of hulled grains,
Ninkasi, you are the one who bakes the bappir in the big oven,
Puts in order the piles of hulled grains,

You are the one who waters the malt set on the ground,
The noble dogs keep away even the potentates,
Ninkasi, you are the one who waters the malt set on the ground,
The noble dogs keep away even the potentates,

You are the one who soaks the malt in a jar,
The waves rise, the waves fall.
Ninkasi, you are the one who soaks the malt in a jar,
The waves rise, the waves fall.

You are the one who spreads the cooked mash on large reed mats,
Coolness overcomes,
Ninkasi, you are the one who spreads the cooked mash on large reed mats,
Coolness overcomes,

You are the one who holds with both hands the great sweet wort,
Brewing [it] with honey [and] wine
(You the sweet wort to the vessel)
Ninkasi, (...)(You the sweet wort to the vessel)

The filtering vat, which makes a pleasant sound,
You place appropriately on a large collector vat.
Ninkasi, the filtering vat, which makes a pleasant sound,
You place appropriately on a large collector vat.

When you pour out the filtered beer of the collector vat,
It is [like] the onrush of Tigris and Euphrates.
Ninkasi, you are the one who pours out the filtered beer of the collector vat,
It is [like] the onrush of Tigris and Euphrates.

Regardless of how, where and when beer was first brewed, it was eventually introduced to Europe from the Middle East. Beer became an integral part of life for northern Europeans, with ample crops needed for brewing. It also was a safe alternative to drinking water, as freshwater was often contaminated with waste runoff. (And the beer was mostly enjoyed by northern Europeans. Southern Europeans, for reasons we won't get into here, tended to enjoy wine instead of beer.)

Beer evolved over time. As anyone who has perused a menu at a modern craft brewery can tell, pretty much anything can go into a beer these days, even beard trimmings—try Rogue Ales' Beard Beer from Ashland, Oregon. In days gone by, that was also true. In the earliest days of beer making, people added ingredients like dates, pomegranates, olive oil and herbs. A sniff and a sip of Midas Touch from Dogfish Head Brewery in Delaware will give you some idea of the ingredients that went into ancient beer. However, our modern (and maybe crumbling) conception of beer owes a lot to Germany's sixteenth-century Reinheitsgebot beer purity laws dictating the use of only water, hops, barley and yeast as acceptable brewing ingredients. You may notice that leaves out ingredients like rice, which is used in a great many beers we know, such as Budweiser and Coors Lite. But, to be fair to these big guys, even the early German immigrants to the United States had trouble following these statutes. The climate in North America was, and is, different than that in central Europe, and this produced a different kind of barley—six-row barley here and two-row barley across the Atlantic. In addition to tasting different than two-row barley, six-row barley also contains a different number of proteins. This meant that Germans brewing in America had difficulty reproducing the clear, golden lagers they loved so much in Europe. Low-protein grains like corn and rice got around this and gave them that coveted clarity.

As German immigrants flooded into the States, beer took off like never before. By 1860, there were nearly 1,300 breweries around the United States. During the Civil War, each barrel of beer had a one-dollar tax added to help local governments finance their militaries.

Breweries from New York led efforts to form an association that would eventually and officially become the United States Brewers Association (USBA). The USBA existed until 1986, when it was reorganized to what is known today as the Beer Institute. The Beer Institute is a national trade association in Washington, D.C., that represents those who produce and import beer in the United States.

Until the twenty-first century, the most breweries operating at one time maxed out in 1871 at 4,131, producing a total of nine million barrels of beer that year. It was around this time that Anheuser Brewery began bottling beer in St. Louis, Missouri, after a discovery by Louis Pasteur that would keep beer fresher, longer. This process became known as pasteurization.

At the turn of the twentieth century, improved methods of production, distribution and regulation of beer brought a decline to the number of breweries around the country. But it also helped improve the quality of the product—that is until Prohibition went into effect in 1920. Many breweries turned to near beer, a no- to extremely-low-alcohol beer.

As the repeal of Prohibition was introduced in 1933, tax on each barrel of beer soared to five dollars. Two months after Prohibition ended, only thirty-one breweries were in operation. Less than a year later, operating breweries grew at a staggering pace, exceeding seven hundred.

The first brewery to put beer in cans was Krueger Brewing Company in Newark, New Jersey, in 1935. Two decades later, the first tall boy sixteen-ounce can was introduced in, you guessed it, Wisconsin by Schlitz Brewing. Canned beer outsold bottled beer for the first time in 1969.

Despite the innovations, the mid-twentieth century was a tough time for local and regional brewing. The population bottomed out after the post-Prohibition boom, in 1983, with a mere eighty breweries making beer across the United States. According to the Brewers Association in 2019, there was a staggering seven thousand breweries in operation around the nation. In 2017, American breweries pumped out 196.3 billion barrels of golden suds. To put that into context, a U.S. beer barrel is measured as 31 U.S. gallons. This equals 6,085,300,000,000 (that's 6 trillion) gallons of beer. That's 48 trillion pints of beer. That's nearly 61 trillion cans of beer.

Just how big of a number is 61 trillion? Let's convert that to something we can understand—beer cans to time. If one can of beer equals one second, how long would it take one person drinking one can of beer each second to finish all of the beer brewed in the United States in 2017: 61 trillion seconds is 1.01 trillion minutes is 17 billion hours is 704 million days is 1.9 million years. That's a long time. That's a lot of beer.

This large number of breweries is attributed to the craft beer boom of the past decade. There are six different segments of craft breweries. Microbreweries must produce fewer than fifteen thousand barrels of beer per year and sell 75 percent or more of their beer off-site through distribution. A brewpub is a restaurant brewery that sells 25 percent of its beer on-site and operates significant food services. A taproom brewery needs to sell at least 25 percent of its beer on-site but does not offer significant food options. A regional brewery brews between fifteen thousand and six million barrels of beer annually. Contract brewing is when a business or brewery hires another to brew beer on its behalf. And finally, alternating proprietor brewing is when one brewery physically takes over another while brewing.

Good beer is good beer, though. Much of the behind the scenes is not a concern of the average consumer. The best beer is the one you enjoy the most, regardless of price, style, location or brewery. Drink what you like. Enjoy what you drink.

I'm here to tell the stories of Green Bay breweries and the history of beer around here.

Part II.

GREEN BAY'S ORIGINAL BREWERIES

BLESCH BREWERY (1851–79)

Since the earliest days of brewing in Green Bay, Francis Blesch boasted good beer at cheap prices. He took out an ad in a local newspaper, the *Green Bay Advocate*, to share that the prices of Bay Brewery were competitive with any other establishment around the country. Blesch even went so far as to publicly guarantee that Blesch beer would be of high quality—a standard the people of Green Bay eventually grew to expect.

How does the first brewery in Green Bay make such an outlandish statement? Sure, he had limited to no competition, but bad beer is bad beer, regardless of the other options. Blesch stood by his beer, and the people of Green Bay finally had their very own suds brewed right in their own town.

Blesch holds the title of first commercial brewer in Green Bay. As was often the case in the early days of breweries, Blesch was a German immigrant. He arrived in Green Bay from Bergen, a small town in Lower Saxony located in the northern part of the country, in 1850 and brought knowledge in the brewing and cooperage trades. Coopering is the trade of making wooden casks and barrels.

Blesch opened Bay Brewery on Pearl Street between Hubbard and Walnut Streets in 1851 on the west side of the Fox River, known then as the town of Fort Howard. Bay Brewery was later called Blesch Brewery and operated until the late 1870s.

Employees pose for a picture before a beer delivery departs, circa 1870. The first brewery in Green Bay was Blesch's Bay Brewery. *Photo courtesy of the Neville Public Museum of Brown County.*

Blesch built his brewery from locally sourced limestone excavated from a quarry at the mouth of Dutchman's Creek. This three-story brewery building was the largest stone construction in Brown County at the time. The proud celebration at the conclusion of construction consisted of firing guns into the air and proudly raising banners a full three stories above the streets of Green Bay.

In a protective approach to fire prevention, Blesch had a state-of-the-art apparatus installed over the Fox River. It consisted of a force pump connected from the brewery building to a pipe running into the river to bring water to the brewery quickly in case a fire broke out. This had all the necessary hoses and pipes to bring the same amount of water as the common hand fire engine of the 1850s. Blesch was hailed as a shining example of what other businesses should do on both sides of the river to take precaution against fire. Should there be fires, they wouldn't be as devastating if the buildings were equipped with this apparatus.

Regardless of the proactive approaches to firefighting, a fire still broke out at Blesch's brewery in 1856. The wooden buildings of the brewery were entirely destroyed. Blesch's residence was also badly scorched. It was suspected that the fire originated from a careless drunken party nearby. The irony that the inebriated partygoers could have been drinking Blesch beer was not overlooked.

Blesch saw much success in that impressive stone brewery. According to the 1860 federal census, Blesch had $7,000 of capital invested in his business. In the storage area, he had three thousand bushels of barley valued at $1,500. Bay Brewery employed four men, who produced one thousand barrels of beer the year prior. These four men each had a monthly wage of $40. That's less than many consumers' monthly beer budgets today.

The 1860s was a significant time of growth for Francis Blesch and his brewing dream. The 1870 census saw a 400 percent increase in capital invested, now totaling $30,000. His barley stash grew to six thousand bushels valued at $6,000. He was now in possession of two tons of hops, valued at $600, and 250 cords of wood, valued at $750. His annual production of beer doubled to two thousand barrels, despite adding only one more employee to the brewing process in ten years. The value of the beer, however, more than tripled to $18,000.

The brewery included an event space to accommodate large groups. Blesch Hall was remodeled to be even larger in 1877 to accommodate larger parties. The entire length of the building became one large hall, used for local association meetings, social gatherings, church benefits, dances and any other functions where people wanted to gather at a brewery. This growth made Blesch Hall one of the largest and most successful businesses in the area. The beer freshly brewed on the premises may have helped.

One particular event held at Blesch Hall was said to have been the most select and fashionable event ever held in Fort Howard. This was a feather in the cap for Mr. Blesch.

In February 1869, a humorous review in the *Green Bay Weekly Gazette* spoke very highly not only of Blesch beer but also of its brewing facility: "Mr. Francis Blesch's 'Bay Brewery' is a model one, situated at Ft. Howard, a large stone building, almost completely covered with creeping vines, on every windowsill choice shrubs worth mints of money. The floors, walls, and ceilings are clean as clean can be. One drinks of his beer with a relish knowing that he is not swallowing unknown amounts of dirt and filth with every glass. The 'Bay Brewery' beer is healthy, and if people would drink only such beer and leave other kinds of drinks alone, much good would be the result." Blesch clearly realized his success was found in the smallest details of his facility, his beer and his curbside appeal. This was setting a high standard for future Green Bay breweries.

Not everyone was impressed with this brewery, though. Officials were cracking down on violations against the city's decency laws. In 1873, Francis Blesch was arrested for illegally selling alcohol on Sundays. This law would have drastically changed football gameday in Green Bay as we currently know it.

To protect the product of his hard work and the infringement on his land, Francis Blesch went to battle with the Chicago & Northwest Railroad. He filed a lawsuit in 1873, claiming the railroad had trespassed on his Fort Howard brewing property. The railroad claimed it was not even touching the edge of the Blesch property. Nonetheless, Blesch was suing for $12,000 in damages. Considerable surveying was conducted to determine exactly where property lines were drawn.

Five years after the lawsuit was filed, in mid-October 1878, Francis Blesch was awarded $3,251 by a jury of his peers to be paid by the Chicago & Northwest Railroad for damages caused by the railroad laying its track in front of his brewing premises.

Not only was Blesch a detail-oriented, standup guy, but he also hired those kinds of men. If this story is any indication of the kind of men Blesch hired, the brewery was surrounded by good, hardworking individuals. This anecdote came from the obituary of Martin Huber. Huber was a German immigrant who arrived in Green Bay a few years after Blesch opened his brewery. His first job in America was working in Blesch Brewery. He eventually left the brewery to become a bartender at a local saloon. Huber finally owned his own saloon after learning how to run one while working for someone else. The *Green Bay Press Gazette* claimed Huber's saloon to be the best-conducted establishment of its kind in the city. Huber was also a fireman—the oldest fireman, in fact—on the local Fire Engine Company No. 1. At a hotel fire in the town of Fort Howard, Huber worked hard fighting the flames and risking his life to ensure the safety of others. His exposure to the blaze caused him to be bedridden for two months. At the age of forty-two, this beloved saloon owner, who was welcomed to this country by the first brewery in Green Bay, was no longer able to entertain people from behind the bar with the brew he loved after losing his life to the injuries endured during this raging fire battle.

Brewing beer didn't seem to be the safest of jobs in the late 1800s. Late nineteenth-century newspaper reporters also seemed to share every little incident that happened around the city. The *Green Bay Advocate* reported of an unfortunate, but ultimately fine, incident for poor Jack Kelleher, an employee of Blesch Brewery. He "got a little tunk on the head" by the breaking of a scaffolding at the brewery while he was packing ice in the cellar. He was knocked unconscious, taken home and cared for. He was ultimately fine. That was it. That's the whole news story.

Another, more serious injury-related story came from Blesch Brewery after a local tavern called for a keg of beer to replenish its stock. Blesch sent one of his workers down to the beer cellar. After not seeing him return for a while, Mr. Blesch heard distressed crying and moans of pain coming from downstairs. He went to investigate and found his worker sprawled on the floor. As the man was carrying the keg of beer up the stairs from the cellar, he was almost to the top when the stairs fell out from underneath him. The beer man broke his leg just above the ankle. As Blesch was trying to assist the young man, Blesch also fell, causing a shoulder injury.

Not only did this brewery see some physical pain but there were also some financial woes. Sometime in early 1876, Blesch Brewery was seized by U.S. deputy collector Luther Buxton for violating regulations of the revenue law. The brewery was then turned over to the U.S. marshals.

Shortly after the seizure of property, the perishable stock was auctioned off. Charles S. Hamilton, U.S. marshal, even took out a personal ad in the *Green Bay Press Gazette*, promoting the sale of this Blesch loot. There were 138 barrels of new beer, 70 barrels of old beer, 300 pounds of hops and 250 bushels of barley. The new beer was sold at $1.50 per barrel. The old beer was sold for $0.05 per barrel. This was $0.05 more than it was appraised at. The beer was supposed to be "good for nothing, old, and sour." Hops brought in $0.01 per pound and barley $0.31. The sale yielded a total of $228.90.

This case of the *United States vs. Francis Blesch* was called to trial at the U.S. Court of Oshkosh in July 1877. The indictment consisted of two counts—one for irregularity in bookkeeping and the other for failing to cancel a beer stamp. Beer stamps were a process used to keep track of taxes owed on beer. Something that looked like a postage stamp was placed over the bung of the barrel. On placement, the brewery needed to cancel the stamp, usually by punching a hole through it, so it could not be reused. When the barrel was tapped at the bung, the stamp was also destroyed to avoid illegal duplicate use. The district attorney filed a discontinuance for the first count. After organizing a jury of six for the second count, the district attorney eventually called for a

Francis Blesch is buried at Fort Howard Memorial Park. This pioneer of beer in Green Bay is located in block E, lot 22, space 8, with an impressive headstone. *Photo courtesy of Cameron Teske.*

discontinuance of this as well, clearing Francis Blesch of any wrongdoing against the U.S. deputy collector. The U.S. marshals then had to turn the brewery over to Mr. Blesch.

Due to health issues, Blesch never reopened the brewery. On the morning of November 10, 1879, Francis Blesch, an old and prominent citizen of Fort Howard, finally succumbed to consumption. The funeral ceremony was held at the family home two days after his death. He was thought to be the wealthiest person in the area at the time of his death.

Francis Blesch left everything to his wife, Antoinette—approximately $33,000 of real estate and personal property. He left very specific instructions on how to handle his farm. It could not be sold within twenty years of his death and must be worked in the same manner as was done while he was alive. The specificity with which Blesch cared about his farm, even in the afterlife, did not carry over to his brewery. As such, the brewery remained closed as it had been since the government seizure in 1876 and following Blesch's health troubles.

The building, which was home to the city's first brewery, sat neglected and vacant for many years. Part of it was demolished in 1898 to make space for J.L. Jorgensen to build three cottages. The other part became a candy company, later turning into an automatic index filing company. The building was completely gutted in a fire in the early 1900s. The famous third story of the once-tallest building in the city was removed in a renovation to the charred building.

At Fort Howard Memorial Park Cemetery, history and beer lovers can pay their respects to Francis Blesch, the pioneer of Green Bay beer, for paving the way for breweries in the city.

HOCHGREVE BREWERY (1865–1949)

In 1853, August Hochgreve immigrated to the United States at the age of twenty-five from his homeland of Hanover, Germany. He landed in New York, where he spent about a year before moving to Wisconsin. In Manitowoc, Hochgreve employed his cooper skills. A cooper is an artisan and woodworker who makes barrels and kegs.

Hochgreve met Henry Rahr, another future Green Bay brewer, while in Manitowoc. They moved north in 1858 to create a joint brewing venture in Bellevue, just a couple miles south of Green Bay. This partnership was called

Bellevue Brewery employees stand in front of August Hochgreve's brewery around 1873. *Photo courtesy of the Neville Public Museum of Brown County.*

Hochgreve beer tray to serve their suds. *Jerry Strebel Breweriana Home Collection, Michelle Van Lieshout Graphic Design and Photography.*

Bellevue Brewery. It lasted until 1865, when Rahr left to build a brewery in Green Bay's city limits.

Now on a solo venture, August renamed the business Hochgreve Brewery but kept the location at 2200 Riverside Drive. August won over the local population with his kind and generous nature. He had been described as an honest man of upright character, who could make many friends.

He once sent a keg of his well-crafted lager to the *Green Bay Weekly Gazette* office. In return, the paper issued a public thank you, claiming it to be "fully equal to the best manufactured beer in Milwaukee." Giving beer to journalists may have been an angle he was playing, but it resulted in even better publicity than he could have anticipated.

Less than five years after Hochgreve Brewery began operation, August already needed major expansions. He built a fourth cellar in 1869 to meet the demand of his increasing beer production. This new cellar was dug well underground to keep the beer at a crisp drinking temperature on hot Wisconsin summer days. This underground "lagering" was a common practice of German-born brewers of the day, as the long cold storage was necessary for the fermentation of crisp, clean lagers. In fact, the German verb *lagern*, from which lager gets its name, means "to store."

A couple years later, Hochgreve again made extensive renovations to the brewery. He spent a lot of money and time ensuring that his brewery was constantly meeting modern standards. A new building that cost $25,000 would be able to pump out seventy-five barrels a day. This required two new cellars to keep the beer cold and fresh while it sat waiting for consumption.

Extremely proud of his product, Hochgreve sent another keg to journalists at the *Green Bay Press Gazette*. It worked once, so it had to work twice. Sure enough, they publicly expressed their gratitude to this "jolly brewer," as they referred to him, for bringing "a keg of his best brewing" into the office. In a tongue-in-cheek claim, they shared their extensive research in drinking it and came to the conclusion that the beer could not have excelled at any point in quality. These reporters also thanked Hochgreve for expanding his brewery so that the beer would never be in short supply.

August Hochgreve suddenly and unexpectedly died in the late winter of 1877. He left his wife, Caroline, and seven children. His obituary could not have spoken any higher of him: "He was a good business man, true and unwavering in his friendships, generous to a fault, and honorable in his dealings." He was a member of the Turners' Society. As a testament to his popularity, Turner Hall flew its flag at half-staff, showing the members' grief over losing such a prominent member. Hochgreve's funeral was the

The Hochgreve Brewing Company property was located at 2200 Riverside Drive in Allouez. The house on the right is the Hochgreve residence, occupied by Twigs Floral today. The bottling house is on the left, which is now an office building. *Photo courtesy of the Neville Public Museum of Brown County.*

largest ever held in Brown County, with hundreds following the processional to Woodlawn Cemetery.

With the loss of their brewing leader, August's wife, Caroline, and son Adolph picked up right where he left off. After just three years under this new duo, the brewery was producing nearly two thousand barrels of Bavarian and Muenchner lager.

Hochgreve Brewery charted the third-largest brewing operation in Green Bay—that is until Prohibition. In May 1924, U.S. marshal Richard White raided Hochgreve Brewery. He found plenty of "good" beer. On the morning of May 12, 2,500 barrels of Hochgreve beer were dumped into the Fox River. Employees and reporters sadly witnessed thousands of dollars' worth of amber foam float downstream.

After the repeal of the Eighteenth Amendment, Hochgreve opened its doors once again under the leadership of Christian Hochgreve. Despite having no practice during the previous decade-plus, the brewery boasted the same brewmaster still brewing the pre-Prohibition favorite mellow beer with the same craftsmanship, care and skill.

Still trying to impress the post–Twenty-First Amendment crowd and fix up a building that hadn't been touched in thirteen years, Hochgreve Brewery spent $75,000 to restore the brewery to its previous standards. This vast update had Hochgreve brewing almost fifty thousand barrels during its height in 1945.

Sadly, sales began declining too rapidly to continue. The Hochgreve family shut down the brewing operation in 1949. A year later, the building housed the Reimer Sausage Company until 1984. It was then renovated to be used as office space.

RAHR BREWERY (1865–1966)

Henry Rahr began the art of brewing beer in his home country of Germany, where he was born on Christmas Day in 1834. He set off to pursue the American Dream at the age of nineteen. Rahr settled in Manitowoc. His passion for beer carried his success in the new country. He worked at a small brewery owned by his uncle in Manitowoc shortly after his arrival in 1853.

Henry Rahr left Manitowoc several years later and found his way north to Green Bay. A partnership between August Hochgreve and Henry Rahr led

A street-level view of the Rahr Brewery. *Photo courtesy of the Brown County Historical Society from the collection of Chuck Golueke.*

to the founding of the second brewing company in Brown County, Bellevue Brewery, in 1857.

After some differences in business practices, Rahr and Hochgreve decided to split ways. They decided to draw straws to see who would remain at Bellevue, located along the banks of the Fox River. Rahr came up on the short end of this gamble.

In 1865, Henry Rahr sold his share of the Bellevue Brewery to August Hochgreve. Rahr ventured off to Green Bay to open his own brewery in the 1317–31 Main Street area between Irwin Avenue and Baird Street. With this proximity to the East River, Rahr named this new production facility the East River Brewery.

The brewery eventually became one of the most successful and longest-operating breweries in Green Bay history. It had humble beginnings, though. The brewing operation employed Rahr and five other men. Rahr served as owner and head brewer. So modest were the early days that brewery employee Jacob Beth claimed he was the entire sales *and* distribution department. His distribution runs consisted of walking down the street with a keg in a wheelbarrow, delivering beer to nearby taverns. The annual production of beer in the beginning was nearly 2,500 barrels.

The original brewing equipment included a steam engine, brewing kettle, beer cellar and icehouse crammed into a two-story stone building of roughly 3,600 square feet. There was also a beer cellar below the building. Rahr and his family lived in part of the brewery, which might sound like a dream come true for many today. But imagine the smells and sounds in a brewery in 1866.

Rahr's East River Brewery also had a malt house, where the team manufactured its own malt to be used in the brewing process. Wet barley was spread across the stone floors in the malt house until it sprouted. This sprouted barley was roasted in a two-story kiln to the proper temperature, and the output was a beautiful malt introduced into the early stages of beer.

Henry Morganstern operated a cooper shop near the East River Brewery. Morganstern supplied Rahr with beautifully manicured wooden kegs made from the locally sourced white oak trees in nearby forests.

A *Green Bay Weekly Gazette* article, dated August 13, 1870, proclaims, "Green Bay is growing; Green Bay is improving rapidly! Growing in wealth, growing in population, growing in commercial importance and all those valuable adjuncts that unite to form a city." So, too, was the brewing industry growing.

By 1880, the Rahr Brewing staff had doubled to ten men. The size of the brewery had also expanded, and new and improved equipment was added. A more powerful twenty-five-horsepower steam engine equipped the brewery to increase production quantity and efficiency. An artesian well was dug to a depth of 150 feet to naturally pump water into the brewery. A fifty-barrel brew kettle was installed to produce five thousand barrels each year.

The icehouse grew to hold about 1,800 tons of ice, which was used for refrigeration in the beer cellars. Ice was thrown over the beer vats to store as close to the desired chilled temperature as possible. During the hot summer months, ice was placed in floating baskets directly into the beer vats.

A horse stable was the newest addition to the brewing process. Two delivery men now distributed the beer using horse-drawn delivery wagons in the summer and sleighs in the winter. The stable housed the dozen-horse delivery crew, along with hay and oats.

The Rahr family still resided in part of the brewery. Mrs. Rahr was a favorite among the brewery employees. She would often bring baskets full of sandwiches for them, made with homemade rye bread and home-smoked ham.

Continuing the family affair, Henry brought his sons, Henry Jr. and Frederick, into the business in 1885. This brought about a name change to Henry Rahr and Sons Brewing Company. Henry Sr. had his sights set on retirement in 1891.

Tragedy struck Henry Rahr and Sons Brewing Company on August 3, 1887. A beer kettle full of seventy barrels of boiling water erupted on seven workers, five of whom died as a result of their injuries on this dark day in Green Bay's history. The *Daily State Gazette* labeled this "the most terrible accident that ever occurred in this city."

The accident occurred during the first brew on a new boiler, which was installed less than a week before the explosion. The workers tested this new boiler to 150 pounds of pressure earlier that afternoon. Seeing that it looked good, they began the regular brewing process. As was their procedure, they boiled between seventy and seventy-five barrels of water around seven o'clock in the evening.

This was a circular boiler built with copper. It had straight sides and a double bottom. The lower bottom portion was made of a specific boiler iron and was riveted to the copper barrel. There was a four-inch space below this iron and the copper through which steam was forced to heat the water to a boil. The whole kettle rested on timbers about five feet from the floor.

Rahr's Brewery workers prepare a delivery of kegs via horse-drawn wagons in 1895. At its peak, Rahr's was producing sixty thousand barrels a year. A barrel equals thirty-one gallons of beer. *Photo courtesy of the Neville Public Museum of Brown County.*

In addition to the rivets, the bottoms were fastened together with five-eighths-inch bolts—no more than the required maximum of six inches apart. The top of the boiler was covered with a board, purposefully not allowing much steam to escape.

In an unrelated project from what was happening in the new boiler, August Delforge, a machinist and engineer, was doing some work on the steam pipes. Delforge's two sons, Frank and Joseph, were helping him on this particular evening. Frank was old enough to have hands-on work with the pipes. Joseph was too young, so his responsibility was to hold a light while the other two worked.

All three Delforge boys were on one side of the kettle. Henry Seifert was in the malt tub on another side of the kettle. Three other men—John Biemeret, George Huber and John Haibe—were on the brewery floor.

At about 8:30 p.m., the pressure of the steam burst the chamber below the kettle, spraying steam throughout the entire room. The kettle was knocked over, throwing at least seventy barrels of boiling water into the air. The room was filled with scalding steam and boiling water several feet deep.

August Delforge was struck in the head by a heavy falling timber that was knocked down by the explosion. He also got the worst of the steam and boiling water as it exploded from the boiler. Foreman Seifert frantically made his way to safety in the boiler room, escaping with one arm slightly burned. The other brewers on the floor ran in the opposite direction, unknowingly into the hottest part of the steam and water.

The Delforge brothers broke through a window and escaped but not quickly enough to avoid being burned by the steam. John Biemeret began making his way to another window but fell into a deeper hole filled with boiling water. "With a desperate leap he reached the window and after leaving the skin of one hand like a glove on the bars was pulled out by men outside the building," wrote the *Daily State Gazette* the following day. John Haibe and George Huber made it out of the front door but eventually succumbed to their scalding injuries. Henry Seifert escaped the malt tub with severe burns that were not fatal.

The explosion was so loud that it brought many neighboring people running to the scene. Everything happened very quickly. It took just moments for the steam and boiling water to dissipate from the room so others could enter and try to rescue anyone who was still inside. August Delforge was found in a pool of blood, unconscious but alive. Delforge was quickly brought outside. Dr. Lewis arrived about half an hour after the explosion and began assessing August Delforge. His skull was fractured, and he was slowly dying. Dr. Lewis did what he could for August, but he knew it was too late.

The doctor began focusing on the others who were in great suffering. Their groans and cries of agony could be heard from a distance. Frank Delforge was the most injured. It took four men to hold him still from his painful thrashing. Opiates were given to soften his pain for a brief reprieve before his charred body gave up. He was no longer in pain.

Eventually, several doctors arrived to help relieve the pain of these men in whatever way they could. Loved ones of the scalded victims hurried to the brewery for a chance to say goodbye. "The agonizing wails of grief mingled with the moans of the dying and their pleadings for help were heartrending," recalled a *Daily State Gazette* reporter. It was a scene anyone would have rather forgotten but couldn't get out of their mind.

The remaining living victims were moved to nearby homes. Henry Seifert and young Joseph Delforge shared an upstairs room, while August Delforge's lifeless body still burned downstairs. Mrs. Delforge mourned the death of her husband. She had not been told of her oldest son's death yet so as not to distract her too much while taking care of her youngest boy.

Frank Delforge's corpse was brought into the same room as John Biemeret. As Biemeret lie restlessly in pain, his wife was desperately fanning him to offer any cooling relief she could. John Haibe was also in this room. He could not stop tossing and turning and moaning. George Huber was taken directly home.

August Delforge died at the age of forty-seven, half an hour after the explosion. Frank Delforge died at the age of twenty at 11:00 p.m. Joseph Delforge died at the age of sixteen, just after 12:00 a.m. John Haibe died at the age of twenty-eight at 2:30 a.m. John Biemeret died at the age of thirty-four around 3:00 a.m.

Henry Siefert was seriously burned but survived the explosion. He was badly scalded on his arms, hands, neck and chest.

On hearing the news, Henry Rahr Sr. was physically ill and terribly devastated.

A memorial honoring the five men who lost their lives as a result of this tragic explosion was erected in the Allouez Catholic Cemetery.

Continuing the devastation surrounding Henry Rahr and Sons Brewing Company, Henry Rahr suffered a fatal heart attack before having the opportunity to enjoy his retirement. He had a reputation of being an honest, kind, humble, spirited gentleman, who would be greatly missed.

Henry Jr. and Frederick ran the brewing operation successfully to its peak in 1895. Both boys grew up around the brewery, watching their father work throughout their childhood. Henry Sr. taught his sons the finest details of the business, preparing them to one day take over, and they did.

Henry Jr. served as brewery manager, while Frederick took the positions of secretary and treasurer. After the brewery turned over to the founder's sons, the business really took off. The financial growth in the first few years after Henry Jr. and Frederick took over was not only a true testament to the quality of training that they received but also to their skill and wisdom in business management.

The Rahr malt business grew by leaps and bounds, as well. Previously just used in their own brewing operations, under the leadership of Henry Jr. and Frederick, Rahr malt was sold and distributed to breweries all over the country. It was recognized for its superior quality over all other malts.

The beer was also making an even bigger name for itself. George Groessl was hired as brewmaster. Groessl had previously worked for Van Dycke Brewing. He brought his beer expertise to Green Bay from Munich, Germany.

With Groessl as brewmaster, Rahr's Brewing Corporation (the new name as of 1915) was pumping out ten thousand barrels a year of some of the finest quality beer throughout northeastern Wisconsin. This was the largest production of beer in the state of Wisconsin outside of Milwaukee. As

A tragedy at Rahr's Brewing in 1887 resulted in the deaths of August Delforge, Frank Delforge, Joseph Delforge, Jean Baptiste Biemeret and Jean Haibe. They are memorialized at this monument in Allouez Catholic Cemetery. *Photo courtesy of Cameron Teske.*

This plaque honors the five men who tragically lost their lives in the steam explosion at Rahr's Brewing in 1887. *Photo courtesy of Cameron Teske.*

Rahr's Brewing was riding the high of its prime, a looming law change was about to throw the dream into disarray.

The brewery ceased operation for the first few years of Prohibition. The Rahr brothers held out as long as they could but sold the business in 1923. The new owners began to make near beer. This was a malted beverage that contained less than 0.5 percent alcohol by volume. In 1929, federal agents shut down the operation for getting a little too close to actual beer.

There was a reorganization among these new owners that included a name change to Green Bay Products Company. Fred Miller Sr., Roy Joannes and Nic Feldhausen began making wort. This nonalcoholic brew was sold in five-gallon cans. With no grounds for objection from the federal government for the creation or sale of wort, the addition of yeast at home created quite the alcoholic transformation. This wildcat beer, as this wort concoction was affectionately known, was sold at roadhouses all around the area. At its core, a roadhouse was an establishment known to supply illegal beer and booze under the guise of serving food or soda.

After the repeal of Prohibition in 1933, Rahr's Green Bay Brewing Corporation, as it was now known, commenced brewing beer. But the exciting legality of alcohol was not enough to keep Rahr's financials in the

A circa 1916 Rahr Brewing Company delivery truck stopped for a photo opportunity at the intersection of Walnut and Washington Streets. *Photo courtesy of the Brown County Historical Society, Felix Matzke Collection.*

Rahr's Brewery Bottling Plant, located in downtown Green Bay at 1317–31 Main Street, packaged Rahr's various brands in preparation for distribution, circa 1955. *Photo courtesy of the Neville Public Museum of Brown County.*

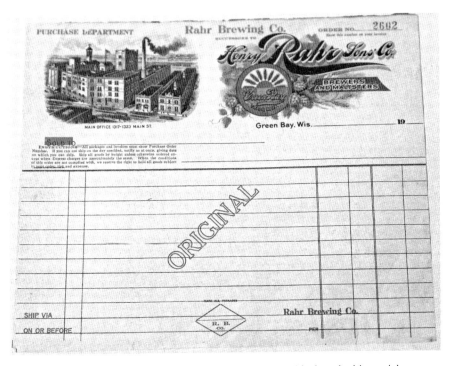

An original Rahr's Brewing Company letterhead featuring a black-and-white aerial overview of the brewery. *Jerry Strebel Breweriana Home Collection, photo by Michelle Van Lieshout Graphic Design and Photography.*

black. A creditors' committee took over the operation, with Frank Tharinger running the plant for a while. In 1935, Fred Miller Sr. acquired complete control of Rahr's Green Bay Brewing.

As major beer brands began to grow and distribution expanded, the local Rahr's Brewery struggled. Thanks to a brewery strike in Milwaukee during the 1950s, Rahr's sales eventually soared once again, albeit for a short time. When that strike was resolved, sales again slowed.

Oshkosh Brewing Company purchased Rahr's Green Bay Brewing in 1966. No new beer was brewed, the lights were shut off and the taps stopped pouring. Green Bay's longest- and largest-running brewery had closed its doors after 101 years in operation.

The entire Rahr's Brewing complex has been torn down. On the grounds that once brewed "the best beer in any case" now resides a BP gas station and a Dairy Queen.

HAGEMEISTER BREWERY (1866–1925)

Francis Hagemeister was the fourth man to try his hand at brewing beer in Green Bay. He left his home country of Prussia in the early 1860s. On arriving to the Green Bay area, Hagemeister opened a prosperous meat market. This endeavor was successful enough that Hagemeister had money to invest in a brewery.

There is no record of Hagemeister having any sort of brewery experience before this. In 1866, he partnered with three other men—Whitney, Mertz and Klaus—to bring this beer idea to life. Together, they opened Union Brewery on Main Street, along Baird Creek, in the town of Preble on Green Bay's east side.

By 1873, Hagemeister had bought out his three partners to become sole owner. This brought a name change from Union Brewery to F.H. Hagemeister Brewing Company.

In 1876, Hagemcister shipped a keg of his best brew to a buddy in Eureka, California. The shipping time to reach the final destination was twenty-eight days. Conrad Englert, the lucky recipient, wrote back to Green Bay commending Hagemeister that the beer, packed in malt, was as fresh as when it started its trek west.

Francis's second-oldest son, Henry, joined the brewing operation in 1882, resulting in a name change to F.H. Hagemeister & Son. This was the peak

A street-level view of the Hagemeister Brewery. Photo courtesy of the Brown County Historical Society from the collection of Dennis Jacobs.

of Hagemeister Brewing. It topped out at five thousand barrels, putting it at the number two spot among Green Bay breweries at the time.

Henry was named president of the brewery in 1886, at the age of thirty-one, after serving as general manager for the past seven years.

Flush with success (and presumably with cash), Hagemeister Brewing purchased the Laidiger Brothers Brewery in Sturgeon Bay, Door County, in 1887. It was originally named Siedman Brewing Company. This $5,000 purchase got Hagemeister the brewery itself, a home, cattle, wagons and sleighs, brewery equipment and accessories and the ten acres of land it all sat on. This investment gave Hagemeister much-coveted control of beer in Door County.

Growth seemed inevitable for the second-largest brewery in Green Bay. A two-story, eight-thousand-square-foot barn was built in connection with the brewery.

After Francis died in 1892, Henry took over Hagemeister Brewing Company. As a slightly twisted nod to the Schlitz slogan, "the beer that

This 1957 aerial photo shows the Reimer's Meat Products Building, which was formerly the Hochgreve Brewing complex on Riverside Drive in Allouez. *Photo donated to the Brown County Historical Society by John Dugan. Photographed by Hank Lefebvre.*

made Milwaukee famous," Henry boasted of his Hagemeister pride with his own pointed slogan: "The beer that made Milwaukee *jealous*." This beloved offering was Hagemeister's Bock Beer. This amber was of superior quality.

Henry also entered politics, elected as an alderman of Green Bay and a Brown County supervisor for nearly a decade. He even rose to president of the county board. The taxpayers of Brown County looked on Henry with favor as a major positive influence on county legislation and area economics beneficial to the people. Henry was eventually elected to state assembly, representing the first district of Brown County, where he again served his constituents well.

As Prohibition loomed, the business changed its name to Hagemeister Food Products Company in order to make ice cream and soda. It unsuccessfully tried to create a healthy alternative soft drink called Cameo. It was made of grains and no sugar, as the ad claimed.

The brewing operation was closed after a raid of the Hagemeister Food Products Company in 1925. Several barrels of "good beer" were seized from a Hagemeister warehouse. Seven people were arrested for their connection to producing and distributing alcohol.

The Hagemeister Brewery's bottling line around 1910. *Photo courtesy of the Brown County Historical Society from the collection of Chuck Golueke.*

Federal Prohibition officials became suspicious of the Hagemeister Company after a thwarted delivery of beer was said to have originated there. After several weeks of surveillance, officials raided the property while several suspicious vehicles were waiting on Hagemeister's loading dock. A Buick Coach contained five half barrels of beer hidden in a space where the back seat was removed. Both license plates had also been removed. The next vehicle waiting for a load was a Studebaker touring car. Searching this car revealed several bottles of red wine and .45-caliber bullets. It was suspected that the gun was thrown into nearby bushes as police arrived, but the weapon was never recovered. A number of kegs filled with beer were also found on the loading dock of the Hagemeister Company.

Several of those arrested were from Michigan's Upper Peninsula (U.P.). It was then suspected that this smuggling ring had been delivering beer to the U.P.

A statement from Hagemeister leaders blamed a new, young employee for these violations. He had recently been hired to operate the soda water department. It was alleged that to impress his bosses and owners with how

The Iron Gate was a Hagemeister Brewery tied house (a tavern that serves a particular brewery's beer) near the current Kroll's East location, circa 1906. *Photo courtesy of the Brown County Historical Society from the collection of Chuck Golueke.*

much money this department brought in, he began selling "good beer." Following the arrests, the soda water operator disappeared.

The brewery operation was stopped following the raid. However, the ice cream, candy and soft drink divisions of Hagemeister could remain open and operating. Hagemeister apparently continued to brew. Just a couple months later, officials returned to Hagemeister. This time, they dumped seven hundred kegs of beer into the Fox River. More arrests were made, and the brewery was officially padlocked.

Compared to the success Hagemeister found in beer, these Prohibition goods just couldn't make ends meet. The Eighteenth Amendment beat out Hagemeister Brewery, when, as Hagemeister Food Products Company, it declared bankruptcy in late 1925. T.P. Silverwood was named trustee of Hagemeister Food Products Company following bankruptcy.

In an attempt at reorganization and resurgence, stock options were offered as Hagemeister Food Products Company began making butter and cheese. These products were suggested because they would eliminate waste created while making ice cream.

Otto's Buffet was a tied house for Hagemeister Brewery. There is a Hagemeister crest at the very top of the building, just below 1892. Otto's Buffet was located on the northwest corner of Main Street and Washington in downtown Green Bay. *Photo courtesy of the Brown County Historical Society, Felix Matzke Collection.*

A football game between the Packers and St. Louis is played at Bellevue Field with Hagemeister Brewery in the background. *Photo courtesy of the Neville Public Museum of Brown County.*

Despite some of the issues following bankruptcy, Hagemeister was progressing just fine. However, in February 1926, Hagemeister Food Products Company was put up for sale to the highest bidder.

Schreiber Foods can now be found in the former Hagemeister Brewing facilities and on the grounds at 1609 Main Street.

VAN DYCKE BREWERY (1876–1908)

To get to Louis Van Dycke and Van Dycke Brewing, we need to start with Sebastian Landwehr and Michael Baier.

In late 1872, the foundation for another brewery in Green Bay had just been poured. This two-story building, plus a basement, was set for a maximum brewing capacity of three thousand barrels per year. This was no small operation.

In July 1873, the exterior of Landwehr's City Brewery was finally finished. Just a month prior, a shipment of casks, kegs and tubs aboard the tugboat *Ajax* floated down the Fox River toward this brewery located on Chicago Street and Jackson Street in downtown Green Bay. The *Green Bay Press Gazette* called for the attention of all "lager-loving citizens" to eagerly anticipate another brand of beer in the area. This site was strategically chosen—there was a fountain of water said to be the best in the area for making high-quality beer.

Brewing began in August 1873 in the largest brewery north of Milwaukee at the time. This steam-powered brewery was advertised as an ideal model of neatness and workmanship. City Brewery was highly esteemed for its solid construction and architectural design. As the largest brewery around, it brewed 1,300 barrels of golden suds. With that kind of output, City Brewery needed a place to keep its beer cool. It installed a beer cooler that was nearly forty thousand cubic feet.

After three months in operation, the first beer out of City Brewery hit the lips of patrons on November 18, 1873.

Unfortunately, a mere seven months after pouring their first mug, Sebastian Landwehr and Michael Baier's beer dreams were foreclosed on. City Brewery's land and building were set to be auctioned off to the highest bidder from Sheriff Crocker's office in October 1876. This three-year endeavor was about to come to an end. City Brewery was originally built at a project cost of $70,000. With such a steep investment, the brewery was never able to turn the books into the black.

Employees of the O. Van Dycke Brewing Company in front of the brewery, circa 1890. Louis Van Dycke originally called the brewery Green Bay Brewery. His wife, Octavia, changed the name to O. Van Dycke Brewing Company after Louis's death in 1881. *Photo courtesy of the Neville Public Museum of Brown County.*

On December 18, 1876, City Brewery officially changed hands to Louis Van Dycke and Charles Berner of Green Bay and two other investors, C. Schwartz and Sylvester Hartman of Fort Howard.

Louis Van Dycke was born in Antwerp, Belgium, on April 15, 1828. He spent his early days following in his father's footsteps as a master of ships. His father, Constante Van Dycke, was of Dutch nobility and was a wealthy sea captain who sailed his own ship all around the world, delivering a variety of shipped goods. Throughout Louis's days as a sea captain, he became quite the linguist, capable of picking up many foreign languages rather quickly.

On arrival to the United States during an influx of Belgian immigration, he originally settled in Kewaunee County in 1855. Two years later, he married Octavia Caesar. Van Dycke is the namesake for the village of Dyckesville, a small town northeast of Green Bay. This recognition was given to him after founding the town and opening a successful general store. He was a well-respected leader in his community and was elected as district attorney. Van Dycke was also appointed as the first postmaster in the region. In those days, roads were few and far between, making deliveries a big deal and the delivery man a favorite among his routes. Louis served as the town treasurer for a decade as well.

Octavia and Louis moved to Green Bay in 1868. Van Dycke had accumulated a considerable amount of property through real estate investments in Green Bay, Menasha, Michigan and a large property in Belgium.

As for the brewery Van Dycke and crew had just purchased, they made a very wise and profitable investment on this property sold under a mechanic's lien. The winning bid at foreclosure auction was a mere $9,500. This group of men became the fifth operation to join in the nineteenth-century Green Bay brewing fun. The group changed the name to the Green Bay Brewing Company.

The property issues for Landwehr and Baier continued into the early part of the year after losing their physical business. To continue paying off their mortgage, their brewing equipment was also auctioned off. All of their eighth barrels, quarter barrels and half kegs were included, along with their beer tanks, mash tuns and all other cooperage paraphernalia in their vaults or storage above the brewery. There was also one large copper kettle that held a capacity of about sixty barrels of beer. These two men were also in default on other brewing equipment purchased as they pursued their beer dreams: one malt grinder, one pitch machine, a beer cooler, a scale, two brass faucets, 120 grain bags, four beer swimmers and one force pump used in the beer cellar. Mortgagee Anton Seibel was about to lose plenty of money on this deal. He, however, meant business and would recover any bit of money possible by selling anything he could after this loan went poorly.

Less than a year after this brewery was purchased at auction, Green Bay Brewing Company had been fixed up to be one of the very best in the state. Van Dycke and Berner had also bought out their partners, Schwarz and Hartmann. In October 1877, brewing commenced in the facilities located on the southwest corner of Jackson Street and Chicago Street in the heart of Green Bay.

More than a year after purchasing the brewery, Van Dycke and Berner were finally ready to give Green Bay a taste of its namesake's beer. George Grissel, an experienced brewmaster, was the mastermind behind the actual brewing process. After spending more than four years working at the local general store, Charles Berner could put his full-time effort into the brewery as he took over the business management.

The *Green Bay Advocate* got an early taste of the beer. Rather than letting on to their reaction of the beer, these journalists left it up to the public to decide how good the brew was. However, they still stood by the fact that this brewery was state of the art and one of the nicest facilities in Wisconsin. This was one of the largest brewing operations outside of Milwaukee. At full capacity, it could pump out five thousand barrels of beer each year.

To prepare for the warm summers, area businesses like Green Bay Brewing Company took advantage of the thick ice covering both rivers running through downtown Green Bay, East River and Fox River. Ice was harvested toward winter's end at about eight- to ten-inch cubes to keep beer cellars cold during the warm summers. This sounds like going green before that was even a concept.

Ice was not guaranteed for the brewing business in the nineteenth century, no matter how much people preferred cold beer. In 1880, Green Bay Brewing Company had not yet secured ice late in the winter to keep the beer cellars cold enough for beer storage. After some negotiations, it all worked out, and the brewery secured a full supply. Warm beer could have made for one angry city.

Even though the original brewery was immaculately built to brew a considerable amount, less than a decade later, Green Bay Brewing Company was ready for an expansion. A building eighteen by twenty-four feet and one story in height was constructed across Chicago Street from the original establishment. This building would hold the bottling plant. A.F. Filim was originally in the cigar business but was tasked with bottling Van Dycke's beer.

Louis Van Dycke was sick for most of 1880. He had traveled to Milwaukee to receive medical treatment and was bedridden for nearly three months before eventually succumbing to complications from a large tumor. He passed away in January 1881.

A very painful tumor on his neck had been present for nearly two years. Doctors disagreed as to its nature, whether it was a cancerous tumor or a tumor of the carotid artery itself. Regardless of the cause, its growth was rapid the last few months of his life, eventually bursting on the inside and poisoning his system.

Van Dycke's obituary, as printed in the *Green Bay Press Gazette*, paints a detailed picture of the wonderful and intelligent man he was:

> *Although modest and unassuming in his manner, Mr. Van Dycke was a thorough scholar, writing and fluently speaking five different languages. He was true, faithful and not unfrequently over-generous toward his friends. His early death will leave a deep and lasting impression of sadness in the circle of his numerous acquaintances.*

He leaves a wife and six children to mourn his loss. His love toward them was a true example of Christian virtue. Always ready to sacrifice his personal comfort to promote their happiness. Only a few moments before breathing his last, and while death had spread its shadow over his eyes, he bid his friends to pass to the next room to attend to the comfort of his wife and children, who were lamenting over his death, adding, "I can now die alone in company with my spiritual advisor."

Louis Van Dycke is buried at Allouez Cemetery.

After the loss of her husband, Octavia took over the brewery business. She changed the name to O. Van Dycke Brewing Company. While Octavia served as proprietor, her two sons, Emile and Julius, conducted the brewing operations. Emile was just eighteen years old when he took over. Several years before his father's passing, recognizing that he would be the heir to the brewery, Emile spent a year living in Milwaukee working at some of the best breweries around to learn the details of the trade. Emile also took a full course at the American Brewing Academy, achieving a diploma certification as master brewer.

Julius, the younger of the two Van Dycke sons, pursued a career as a pharmacist before joining Emile at the family brewery. Julius received his pharmacy degree from the University of Wisconsin–Madison. His role at the brewery was to manage the finances. The brewery saw much financial success with Julius at the helm of the books.

Octavia was a tough woman. A story states that she accidentally stabbed her finger with a needle while doing some work one afternoon. As she was trying to remove the needle herself, it broke off in her finger. She was in excruciating pain while she calmly waited for Dr. Brett to arrive and extract the broken piece from her hand.

One winter morning several years after Octavia took over operations, she entered the brewery office to find it in complete chaos. A window was broken, and several other things were damaged. Documents, drawers and anything that could have been rummaged through appeared to have been. The door of the safe had been blown off. It was determined that approximately $150 was stolen from the safe.

A neighbor near the brewery, J.M. Franssens, heard some loud noises in the middle of the night. He assumed that it was something coming from the horse barn and dismissed it. After hearing what happened at Van Dycke's, he regretted not doing something about it at the time. He believed the noise was the explosion to open the safe.

Octavia and her sons pushed the O. Van Dycke Brewing Company to its peak in the mid-1880s, when they were brewing in excess of ten thousand barrels annually. A thorough brewery remodel was also completed, in which a cold storage warehouse, washhouse and racking room were added. A nice new business office was also built.

Unfortunately, just two decades later, O. Van Dycke Brewing Company brewed its last batch in 1908. Hochgreve Brewing Company purchased O. Van Dycke Brewing Company for $45,000. Hochgreve went on to sell the Van Dycke property to the Annen Candy & Biscuit Company, which had outgrown its facility. This brewery space was ideal for Annen to install the most modern—at the time—factory equipment for the manufacture of candy and crackers. The Annen Candy & Biscuit Company was the official supplier of crackers for all of the state institutions.

Part III.

PROHIBITION

A dark age in American history saw the implementation of a constitutional ban on the production, importation, transportation and sale of intoxicating liquors.

Two conversation topics that can turn contentious and are therefore frowned on are politics and religion. So, what the hell, let's talk politics and religion. Feel free to take a quick break to grab another beer.

A wave of religious revivalism during the mid-1800s led to some small movements and calls for temperance—the act of abstinence from alcohol. Some states even passed small versions of the great Prohibition Act. Many lasted only, thankfully, a short time.

The Prohibition movement was led by Protestant Christians at the turn of the twentieth century. Societies espousing a temperate lifestyle formed across the country. Women played a pivotal role, as they saw alcohol as a destructive force in marriages and families. Many factory owners were also in favor of banning alcohol in hopes that it would prevent accidents and increase worker efficiency. Individuals in both the Democratic and Republican Parties bought into this crusade against alcohol. Morality and health benefits drove "drys" to support this drastic nationwide noble experiment.

Andrew Volstead, a Republican U.S representative from Minnesota, managed the legislation for the national Prohibition Act. This led some to call the legislation the Volstead Act. In Wisconsin, can we all agree that of course Prohibition was Minnesota's fault? In Minnesota's defense, though, Volstead was defeated in the election immediately following this debacle of an idea in 1921.

President Woodrow Wilson even vetoed the bill but was overridden by a congressional vote in twenty-four hours, making this bill a law. Intoxicating liquor at 2.5 percent alcohol by volume (ABV) was officially banned across the country. The Eighteenth Amendment was ratified by 75 percent of states in January 1919. Prohibition officially went into effect the following year with the passage of the Volstead Act.

A side effect of Prohibition was violent organized crime. Authorities may have expected some illegal activities but definitely did not anticipate it to be as prominent or problematic as it was. Only a mere 134 agents were initially designated to the Prohibition unit to enforce the laws throughout Illinois, Iowa and Wisconsin.

Those who wanted to continue drinking found clever ways to get their booze. The illegal manufacturing and selling of liquor was known as bootlegging. Speakeasies—stores, shops and nightclubs that sold alcohol—became frequent spots for the affluent. The lesser-quality homebrew was known as moonshine or bathtub gin. Illegal drinking activities ran rampant throughout the entire Prohibition era.

Bars and taverns appeared to have shut down, but they actually just moved "underground." These speakeasies were operated by organized crime members, often referred to as gangsters, the likes of Al Capone, Bugs Moran and Baby Face Nelson. The year between ratification and enforcement gave many of these groups opportunities to stash alcohol in preparation to sell it at steeply inflated prices. Many other gangsters of the era were responsible for massive smuggling rings of booze into the United States.

With the exception of Milwaukee County, Brown County had the most liquor law violations and collected the most fines of anywhere in the state during the first six months of 1925. The following year, Clark Perry, the former Prohibition director of Wisconsin, pleaded guilty to charges of conspiracy to violate the Prohibition laws.

Those who stepped up in opposition to Prohibition were Catholics and German Lutherans. Wisconsin had its fair share of both religious followings. Wisconsin was considered a wet state, and Brown County was a wet county. Frank Buckley of the Bureau of Prohibition wrote a 1929 report called *A Prohibition Survey of the State of Wisconsin*. Buckley began by summarizing the situation around the state: "[Wisconsin is] sort of a Utopia where everybody drinks their fill and John Barleycorn still holds forth in splendor. From the standpoint of actual votes and present conditions, Wisconsin is undoubtedly a wet commonwealth."

Buckley went on to say that liquor had always been plentiful in Wisconsin. He set a scene in Brown County full of prostitution, gambling and other vices that flourished openly. There were also plenty of soda parlors. Practically all of the soda parlors were known to flow with beer, whiskey and moonshine.

During the thirteen years of outlawed liquor, eighty-four "soft drink parlors" popped up throughout the Green Bay area. Buckley described the city of Green Bay as obviously unsatisfactory in regard to following Prohibition laws. It was well known that beer, whiskey and moonshine were flowing at many of these soft drink parlors. In 1928, the year before this report, federal agents raided sixty-two of those soda parlors, forty-nine of which were ultimately shut down for violations.

By city ordinance, no window curtains could be hung anywhere soft drinks were sold. Clever establishment owners installed high-powered lights that would shine so brightly into the eyes of an onlooker that they were unable to see inside.

Buckley also made the bold allegation that the Brown County sheriff was inactive and uncooperative where Prohibition matters were concerned. To make it even harder for Prohibition to stand a chance of success in Green Bay, the city council passed a resolution condemning federal forces for interfering with the way things were done locally. It was basically an official stance of "leave us alone."

Arrests in Green Bay were compiled in Buckley's report during the years 1918, 1928 and 1929. Authorities saw a rise in crime. In 1918, 315 people were arrested for drunken incidents. Just over a decade later, there were 475 arrests in 1929. Green Bay's arrests for other violations grew considerably: 810 in 1918 and 1,180 in 1929. Also in 1929, throughout Wisconsin's Eastern District, agents seized 294 stills, 18,255 gallons of spirits and 56,724 gallons of malt liquor.

A legal alternative to alcoholic beverages during Prohibition was a malt beverage containing less than 0.5 percent ABV, often referred to as near beer. However, it could not legally be labeled as beer and was therefore called a cereal beverage. A popular illegal practice was to add alcohol to bottles of near beer. This was called needle beer because a needle was used to inject alcohol through the cork of the bottle or keg.

President Herbert Hoover, a strong supporter of the Eighteenth Amendment, established the National Commission on Law Observance and Enforcement in 1929. It was also called the Wickersham Commission. The Wickersham Commission was charged with surveying the United States criminal justice system as it related to Prohibition. This eleven-member group then made recommendations for public policy. Much of the investigation focused on alcohol violations and related criminal activity. There was a discovery of corruption among police departments, local politics and other community leaders. The Wickersham Commission took two years to complete its report. Due to the widespread negative effects Prohibition had on American society, the Wickersham Report recommended much more aggressive and extensive law enforcement practices to moderate compliance with the anti-alcohol laws in effect.

Only one of the eleven members refused to sign the report. Monte M. Lemann had a different opinion that the only conclusion to stop the violent crimes was to repeal the Eighteenth Amendment. Repeal did not happen for several more years. Therefore, there was a promise from federal agents to "dry up" Green Bay.

It's no surprise that a Wisconsin senator was responsible for the liberation from a decade-long national dry spell. John Blaine, a former governor of Wisconsin turned Republican senator, served as chairman of a subcommittee of the Senate Judiciary Committee that held hearings addressing the modification of the Volstead Act and ultimate repeal of the Eighteenth Amendment. The Blaine Act was formally called the Joint Resolution Proposing the Twenty-First Amendment to the United States Constitution. President Franklin Delano Roosevelt supported the repeal of Prohibition.

Thanks to Senator Blaine, Prohibition ended in 1933. Senator Blaine introduced the joint resolution on February 20, 1933. Leave it to Wisconsin to bail the country out of a government-mandated dry spell. Join me in raising an alcoholic toast to Senator Blaine, for without him, we might be toasting with near beer or water.

As a result of Prohibition, Americans were introduced to lighter flavored beer. Even after the repeal of Prohibition, this light beer became a popular choice of beer drinkers. Food writer Waverly Root said of this light near beer, "[It was] such a wishy-washy, thin, ill-tasting, discouraging sort of slop that it might have been dreamed up by a Puritan Machiavelli with the intent of disgusting drinkers with genuine beer forever."

Part IV.

PRELUDE TO A CRAFT BEER BOOM

The decades between the repeal of Prohibition and the rise of homebrewing and craft brewing in the 1980s were dark days for local and regional brewers across the nation. Many of the breweries operating prior to the Eighteenth Amendment sprang back to life after the passage of the Twenty-First Amendment. But most would not survive.

The Great Depression began in 1929 and ended during the final year of Prohibition. It appeared as though beer would play a role in saving the national economy. But just when it looked like things were getting better, the United States was pulled into World War II. This one-two punch of economic depression and total war left the beer industry staggering well into the mid-twentieth century, when different forces would put many local and regional brewers down for the count.

Following a nationwide trend of mass culture and mass-produced goods and brands, American brewing suffered—yes, suffered—a relentless onslaught of closures and consolidations as larger breweries bought other smaller breweries. For all of the talk, often with roseate nostalgia, of postwar prosperity, it was this very prosperity that left the American beer industry a largely uniform color—the pale straw hue of a light lager, of course. The growth of the national infrastructure by the 1950s meant that a single factory could send its goods to all forty-eight continental states—a feat unimaginable even in the wildest dreams of most nineteenth-century brewers and manufacturers. Additionally, the amazing success of television allowed mid-twentieth-century companies an unprecedented reach when it came to advertising. These twin forces of transportation and media created, for the first time, a mass consumer culture. Many of the brands that went national at this time are still with us: Coca-Cola, Kellogg's Corn Flakes, Tide laundry detergent and Budweiser.

The famous and ubiquitous American beers Miller Lite, Bud Light and Coors Light were products of this mid-twentieth-century mass consumer culture. In fact, were it not for the piles and piles of cash these national brewers put into 1970s advertising campaigns that ran coast to coast, it's unlikely that these lite lagers would have displaced their local and regional cousins.

These might have been tough times if you were a small brewer making your beer for a local or perhaps regional market. But they were successful days for the big boys. Between 1984 and 1990, the national market share of Anheuser-Busch, Miller and Coors—the three largest brewers in the United States—swelled from a combined 64 percent to 81 percent. Though the aforementioned advances in distribution are partly responsible, advertising deserves most of the credit. By the mid-1980s, these breweries spent close to three dollars in advertising for every keg of beer they produced, and regional breweries simply could not compete. After all, the likes of Anheuser-Busch, Miller and Coors spent more on a single Super Bowl ad than the entire annual advertising budget for regional brands.

You might recall that Rahr's Green Bay Brewing was one victim of consolidation when, lagging mid-century, it was bought out and eventually shuttered by Oshkosh Brewing Company in 1966.

This is how once-regional brands became nationwide (and now worldwide) breweries by those names we all know. The numbers are stunning. In the late 1800s, there were more than four thousand American breweries. By the late 1970s, fewer than one hundred remained. Mercifully, changes were afoot that would liberate the American palate from the same old, same old.

With changes to laws, homebrewing became a passion for many in the 1970s and '80s. At first, this was just a hobby. But eventually, the curiosity of these homebrewers—explorers of foreign and long-forgotten beer styles—coalesced into a full-fledged craft beer boom. The story was pretty much the same across the United States. In Green Bay, like so many other American cities riding a boozy wave of craft beer, the phenomenon started in the home.

Part V.

HOMEBREWING IN GREEN BAY

The Green Bay Rackers Homebrew Club has a tagline on its website: "If you want it done right, you have to brew it yourself." This is a little tongue in cheek but has some truth. There is plenty of pride in the air at downtown Green Bay's House of Homebrew. Not boastful pride but rather pride in the details, the science and the art of the hobby among those who walk in, hang out and work there.

A homebrewing club in Green Bay dates to 1982, when the Green Bay Grain Exchange was founded by members and customers of Life Tools Adventure Outfitters Co-Op, including owner John Hermanson. This store was a place to buy camping, hiking and outdoors gear, as well as, eventually, homebrewing gear—you know, all the major necessary life tools. Life Tools opened in 1977 at 1035 Main Street and moved to Waube Lane, where The Heel Shoe Fitters is today, in the late 1990s. It remained there until 2004, when it closed its doors.

Homebrewing was federally, and finally, legalized in 1978. (Thanks, in large part, to President Jimmy Carter and his brother Billy, a brewer who was known to enjoy a good beer every now and then—and then again and again.) Individual states had, and still have, the right to regulate their own statutes related to homebrewing. It wasn't until 2013 that homebrewing was legally permitted in all fifty states. Many states still prevent homebrewers from removing their own beer from their home. This restricts interactions with the rest of the homebrew community. According to Gary Glass, director of the American Homebrewers Association, "Sharing and community interaction are key ingredients of homebrewing." Homebrewing clubs are an important and enjoyable part of the process.

The Green Bay Grain Exchange first met at the local musicians' union hall. Many founding members of the brew club were also members of the musicians' union. The meetings took place one Saturday each month and consisted of specific brewing topic demonstrations or discussions. Members also tasted homebrews and rare import beers. It was a group full of camaraderie, where members could help other members through hiccups in the homebrewing process and bounce new ideas off one another.

Under the presidency of Bert Zelten in the early 1990s, the club rebranded to the Green Bay Rackers. "Racking" in homebrewing is the process of siphoning liquid from one vessel to another throughout the brewing process. The name also has a nice ring to it, with the rhyming of the local football team.

In 1995, the Green Bay Rackers held its first organized homebrewing competition. Only members could enter their American-style pale ale for this single-style contest. Mike Conard judged this contest. He was the only judge in northeast Wisconsin at the time who was certified through the Beer Judge Certification Program (BJCP).

This contest became an annual event. In its third year, entries expanded to include all BJCP styles, of which there are thirty-four, according to the BJCP Beer Style Guidelines, 2015 edition. Titletown Brewing Company became the host site of this event, which brought a renaming to the Titletown Open Homebrew Competition. There are now about one hundred entries in a variety of styles.

The House of Homebrew was opened in 2004 by Bob Franklin and Bill Widmer and was dedicated to everything a homebrewer may need. The store has since expanded to include tools, equipment and products necessary for making wine and cheese at home, as well. Doug Feck and John Parsons purchased the store in 2018. John Parsons is the current president of the Green Bay Rackers.

There are two basic styles of homebrewing: all-grain brewing and extract brewing. The difference has to do with how the sugars are brought into the process. All-grain brewing is more complex because there is an additional first step. The brewer must convert the starches of malted grains into fermentable sugars through a process known as mashing. In extract brewing, this process has already been done, and the brewer must just add the mash syrup or powder to water to create the necessary wort. Extract brewing is often the process for homebrewers who are just starting out. Neither process

Rahr's beer can labels display the all-star brand. *Jerry Strebel Breweriana Home Collection. Photo courtesy of Michelle Van Lieshout Graphic Design and Photography.*

Rahr's beer bottles with the famous Old Imperial label, boasting the pride of Wisconsin. *Jerry Strebel Breweriana Home Collection. Photo courtesy of Michelle Van Lieshout Graphic Design and Photography.*

Local breweriana collector Jerry Strebel showcases his collection of Rahr Brewery beer cans and bottles. *Jerry Strebel Breweriana Home Collection. Photo courtesy of Michelle Van Lieshout Graphic Design and Photography.*

The Rahr's bottle lineup shows the variety of beers offered in bottles: Wisconsin Belgian Brew, Holiday Brew, Bock Beer, a Green Bay–branded beer and Old Imperial Pale Beer. *Jerry Strebel Breweriana Home Collection. Photo courtesy of Michelle Van Lieshout Graphic Design and Photography.*

Rahr's Old Imperial Pale Beer was sold in seven-ounce bottles, resulting in the nickname Little Imp. *Jerry Strebel Breweriana Home Collection. Photo courtesy of Michelle Van Lieshout Graphic Design and Photography.*

Hochgreve Brewing bottles show an emphasis on Bavarian-style lagers and the traditional bock beer. *Jerry Strebel Breweriana Home Collection. Photo courtesy of Michelle Van Lieshout Graphic Design and Photography.*

Van Dycke beer tap handle has a not-so-subtle message for indecisive patrons: You like Van Dyck Beer. *Jerry Strebel Breweriana Home Collection. Photo courtesy of Michelle Van Lieshout Graphic Design and Photography.*

Rahr's beer tap handles. *Jerry Strebel Breweriana Home Collection. Photo courtesy of Michelle Van Lieshout Graphic Design and Photography.*

Rahr's Old Imperial tap handle. *Jerry Strebel Breweriana Home Collection. Photo courtesy of Michelle Van Lieshout Graphic Design and Photography.*

Rahr's advertisement featuring two outdoorsmen. Rahr's quips that it is "the best beer in any case." Even on a fishing boat, the beer is "sealed in flavor." *Jerry Strebel Breweriana Home Collection. Photo courtesy of Michelle Van Lieshout Graphic Design and Photography.*

"Van Dycke," dated 1908, can be seen in the stone at the top of the former Ten O One Club. *Photo courtesy of Cameron Teske.*

Badger State Brewing frequently rotates its taps and welcomes guest beers. You'll consistently have a great but different experience each visit. *Photo courtesy of Badger State Brewing Company.*

Enjoy your local pour in the Badger State Brewing dog-friendly outdoor beer garden. *Photo courtesy of Badger State Brewing Company.*

Wisco Disco is Stillmank Brewery's flagship beer and most award-winning brew. *Photo courtesy of Stillmank Brewing.*

Hinterland Brewery's former location in downtown Green Bay had a mural logo on the side of the building. This building is now where Copper State is brewing and serving beer with a similar logo mural. *Photo courtesy of Hinterland Brewery.*

Titletown Brewing was located in a former Chicago & Northwest Railroad train depot building until consolidating operations to the Tap Room across the parking lot in early 2020. Enjoying a pint on Titletown's roof patio while a train rolls by allows patrons to reminisce on the history of the building. *Photo courtesy of the Greater Green Bay Convention and Visitors Bureau.*

The Copper State Brewing Company logo, as displayed on the back of the bar, consists of a copper-colored mosaic hop in the shape of the state of Wisconsin. *Photo courtesy of the Greater Green Bay Convention and Visitors Bureau.*

A westward view of Copper State Brewing Company's brewpub located on the corner of Dousman and Broadway in downtown Green Bay. *Photo courtesy of the Greater Green Bay Convention and Visitors Bureau.*

Badger State Brewing glassware proudly filled with the final product after cooking to perfection in those background barrels. *Photo courtesy of the Greater Green Bay Convention and Visitors Bureau.*

This cargo container turned outdoor taproom sits in Badger State Brewing's beer garden, ready to pour some outdoor beers. *Photo courtesy of the Greater Green Bay Convention and Visitors Bureau.*

Badger State Brewing offers a variety of its beers in sixteen-ounce cans. You can purchase these at the taproom and throughout area liquor and grocery stores. *Photo courtesy of the Greater Green Bay Convention and Visitors Bureau.*

A large State of Wisconsin flag hangs in the brewing area at Badger State Brewing as a nod to the namesake and a showcase of their state pride. The state motto included on the flag is "Forward." This is also the mindset at Badger State Brewing. *Photo courtesy of the Greater Green Bay Convention and Visitors Bureau.*

Hinterland's new location in the Titletown District, just across the street from Lambeau Field. *Photo courtesy of Travel Wisconsin.*

Noble Roots' slogan, "Drink Deep," encourages you to savor the beer you're holding, the people around you and the time you have to do so. *Photo courtesy of Noble Roots Brewing Company.*

Noble Roots's origins in homebrewing tradition started with Marv (Hopmeister) and Tyler (the Pioneer) and grew to involve much of the family, including Alex (the Professor), Jordan (the Experimenter) and Luke (Twin Cities Brewer). When the brewery opened, the aprons commemorated their individual contributions. *Photo courtesy of Noble Roots Brewing Company.*

A colorful variety of Hinterland beers served on a six-flight board. Flights are customizable and a great way to enjoy multiple beers. *Photo courtesy of Greater Green Bay Convention and Visitors Bureau.*

Stillmank Brewing Company's logo displayed in the token green and gold colors of Green Bay. When discussing logo design, Brad Stillmank requested a character. The brewer holding a mash paddle worked well. *Photo courtesy of the Greater Green Bay Convention and Visitors Bureau.*

The Stillmank Brewing Company crew enjoys beers in the outdoor seating area during the warm months in Wisconsin. *Photo courtesy of the Greater Green Bay Convention and Visitors Bureau.*

Stillmank's Tailgater English Blonde Ale is brewed with a splash of local apple cider juice, adding a wonderfully crisp and refreshing finish. This beer is great for tailgating at summer baseball games or winter football games. *Photo courtesy of the Greater Green Bay Convention and Visitors Bureau.*

Hinterland's custom tap handles are constantly changing as new beers are brewed and seasonal beers are rotated. *Photo courtesy of the Greater Green Bay Convention and Visitors Bureau.*

Titletown Brewing Company's brewery and taproom are across the parking lot from the former train depot. This is part of the Rail Yard Innovation District in downtown Green Bay. The Rail Yard is a dense, urban, walkable development containing commercial and retail spaces, restaurants and residential options. The overall focus is on innovation and technology. *Photo courtesy of the Greater Green Bay Convention and Visitors Bureau.*

A broader look at the Rail Yard Innovation District. Note Titletown Brewing's Roof Tap, its rooftop patio with beautiful views of downtown Green Bay and the Fox River. *Photo courtesy of the Greater Green Bay Convention and Visitors Bureau.*

is right or wrong or better or worse. It just depends on how complex the homebrewer wants the process to be.

So why do people homebrew? There can be an assumption that it will be cheaper to brew your own beer. It probably won't be. There can be a hope that it will be easy. It definitely won't be and can be filled with plenty of frustration. Homebrewing is often just a very skilled hobby with delicious results. Drinking your first successful brew has quite a sense of accomplishment. You may never have had a beer as good as that one—not because it's better than any other beer but because this beer has your hard work, time, energy and brainpower brewed into it.

Homebrewers also enjoy the freedom and creativity of designing their own recipes. After the process is mastered, it can be fun to experiment with new styles, new flavors and new recipes. There are still beer purists in the homebrewing scene, but there are also plenty of out-there brews. A Green Bay Rackers member, for example, makes beet beer. To each his own.

If you have any interest in becoming a homebrewer, there are plenty of resources in the Green Bay area. The American Homebrewers Association recognizes the first Saturday in November as Learn to Homebrew Day. Each year, the Green Bay Rackers host an event for beginners to introduce them to the art and science of homebrewing.

Whether a homebrewer needs the first piece of equipment or advanced options, the House of Homebrew has anything and everything necessary. The employees at House of Homebrew are passionate about their delicious hobby and are excited to share information and advice with anyone who walks through their doors. John Parsons recommends purchasing an equipment kit. This comes with all of the basic hardware, sans bottles, for a new brewer to make his or her first batch.

Green Bay Rackers members receive a discount at House of Homebrew. They also get one free entry into the annual Titletown Open as a way to show off, gain experience and receive critique. Club meetings are also a great way to learn from experienced homebrewers. Several Green Bay Rackers members have even gone on to become professional brewers—a couple currently operate breweries in the Green Bay area.

There are an estimated 1.1 million homebrewers around the country, producing nearly 1.4 million barrels of beer a year. This makes up 1 percent of all United States beer production.

Part VI.

TODAY'S GREEN BAY BREWERIES

Titletown Brewing Company

*A championship brewing operation with a nod to its hometown
championship football city.*

Brent Weycker is a Green Bay guy through and through. He grew up on the city's west side, attended Green Bay West High School and stayed in the area to attend St. Norbert College. Growing up in Green Bay, Brent enjoyed family outings to his great-uncle's drive-in root beer stand, Barney's Drive In. His grandmother then bought Sno-Cap Drive In during the 1960s, and they made their own root beer. Brent credits these great family members for his entrepreneurial spirit and love for food.

As a college student, Brent discovered his love for classic American beer—Blatz, Schlitz, Miller and Budweiser. Green Bay did not have a big craft beer scene in the late 1980s, when he was attending school. At the time, Sierra Nevada and Sam Adams were the adventurous beers to drink. According to Brent's memory, even Coors fell into this category, as it was all the way from the Rocky Mountains.

On a family vacation after college graduation in 1992, Brent was paging through an inflight magazine and stumbled on an article about brewing beer. This sparked interest in a new hobby. After the trip, he started researching homebrewing. His first brew was a porter. It was drinkable. He enjoyed the process, so he kept going.

As a self-proclaimed history buff, Brent knew that Green Bay had quite the prolific brewing history. Brent had a new dream to bring brewing back to Green Bay. He didn't want a brewery just anywhere in Green Bay; he wanted to find a historical building and repurpose it into a brewery.

When there's a bright idea, as Brent would find out, turning to family is a successful way to go. His oldest sister lived in Chicago with her husband, John Gustavson. Brent's brother-in-law was pursuing his master of business administration. He was required to write a business plan for a class project. After mentioning this to Brent, Brent suggested that this project focus on a plan for a brewpub. This was the real start of the pie in the sky dream of opening up one of their own.

Brent was working in the management program for Walmart, his first real job out of college. After several years, it became apparent that to move up in the company, he would have to move around the country. Brent loved Green Bay. He didn't want to go anywhere else.

As the brewpub idea grew, it became a legitimate reason to stay in the area.

Weycker joined the Brewers Association before ever owning anything other than his homebrew kit. He attended a conference in Oregon that would change the rest of his life for the better. Before flying there, he had some business cards printed up that listed Titletown Brewing Company as his own. This didn't even officially exist yet. Brent was living the old saying "fake it until you make it."

As Brent would find out, the brewing community is a great group of people who are happy to share some information and see another guy get off the ground. Going out to Oregon with just a dream and a business plan was one of the best decisions he ever made.

Brent met some guys in an elevator at the conference who were looking to start a brewery in New York. They were on their way to meet a man named John Hickenlooper of Wynkoop Brewing Company out of Denver, Colorado. Hickenlooper was looking to invest in starting new breweries around the country. Hickenlooper had a knack for start-up craft breweries.

Brent was invited to this meeting with Hickenlooper. He didn't hesitate to join them. Hickenlooper, a Philadelphia native, thought Green Bay was a mystical huge city in the Midwest. He grew up during the Vince Lombardi era, when Lombardi was a larger-than-life, legendary Green Bay Packers coach. Hickenlooper eventually took a trip to the Green Bay area for a wedding and realized it was just a nice, small community with a warm hometown feel to it. It's a place full of charm and character. This perception helped shape Weycker's pitch of a brewery in Green Bay. Hickenlooper was intrigued.

Not too long after this Oregon conference, Gustavson had a layover in Denver. He met up with Hickenlooper and convinced him to take a trip to Green Bay to experience this brewing vision in person. Over a local dinner, they shared the business plan for their brewing operation dream. Straight out of a movie negotiation, Hickenlooper drew up an agreement on a bar napkin and consummated a deal to help these guys figure out how to, once again, start making beer in Green Bay.

With this partnership came funding, knowledge and legitimacy. They actually started to believe this could really happen. At this time, Wynkoop Brewing was a large and successful microbrewery with nearly a decade under its belt. It was located in lower downtown Denver—once a very similar neighborhood to what Green Bay's Broadway District was in the early 1990s. Wynkoop also repurposed a historic building. It served as a spark for growth and development in that area.

Weycker and Gustavson started exploring historic buildings in downtown Green Bay that they could envision being transformed into a brewpub. Weycker would like to say it was love at first sight, but he had his eye on twenty-three acres of an old run-down vegetable canning plant and polluted railyard. It wasn't pretty, but it definitely had potential. Fixing this space also served as a catalyst for the renaissance of the Broadway District.

After the Hickenlooper investment deal was finalized, the old train depot on that twenty-three acres became available for purchase. The Chicago & Northwest Train Depot was built in 1898 on the site of a former Civil War military fort, Fort Howard. The clock tower for the depot was one of the most recognizable landmarks in downtown Green Bay. It's still there today. Eager travelers hopped aboard this train to head to Chicago. Football fans sent off their beloved team to road games. Families watched as their loved ones left for war. They eagerly welcomed them back home when the fighting was done. This train depot held many emotions and memories for many people.

The railroad still owned the land and was going to sell to the city. The city was looking for a developer who could make this into a booming area again. It sent out requests for proposals. The highest bidder with the best plan for revitalization would ultimately win the opportunity to purchase and develop the land.

That just so happened to be Weycker and Gustavson's Titletown Brewing Company project.

There was a new opportunity on the horizon full of happiness and gathering over a pint or a bite. Titletown Brewing Company walked into a one-hundred-year-old train depot with a plan to revitalize it. When they purchased the building, it had been vacant for many years. It had some wear and tear, but overall, it was kept in tolerable condition. Weycker and crew got to work transforming this space into a brewpub.

Titletown Brewing Company opened its doors on December 6, 1996. Head brewmaster Jim Olen's beer was flowing that day, and patrons were loving it. The first brew on tap was Johnny Blood Red. This red ale's name can be linked back to a historically beloved Packers player, Johnny "Blood" McNally. It was only appropriate that Titletown Brewing Company's first beer honored the championship team that brought the city its nickname and this brewery its namesake.

Johnny Blood Red took home a silver medal in the category of Irish-style red ale at the 2015 Great American Beer Festival. This event, held annually in Denver and hosted by the Brewers Association, is the largest ticketed beer festival in the United States and one of the largest beer festivals in the world. As far as American beer festivals go, it's practically the Super Bowl, the World Series and the NBA Finals rolled into one. That's quite an honor for a local brewer.

Many other beers have special stories behind their names. It is a local brewery that gives recognition to locals. Titletown wanted to pick names that meant something to the community. Another original beer was the 400 Honey Ale. Four hundred was the railroad line number for the Chicago & Northwest route between Green Bay and Chicago. These beers are still two of their best sellers.

Bridge Out Stout was a tongue-in-cheek reference to the Main Street bridge in downtown Green Bay that brought east siders to Titletown. It was closed for construction during the first four years Titletown was open. The Boathouse Pilsner was named for the first true pilsner Brent ever had in Prague, Czech Republic, at a place called the Boathouse. Titletown takes the Green Bay water, adds minerals and takes some out to give it exactly the same content as the water used to brew beer in Pilsen, Czech Republic. True geeky beer drinkers know the importance of water to beer. Befitting the Titletown moniker, the Boathouse Pilsner took home the gold medal in the Bohemian-style Pilsner category at the 2010 Great American Beer Festival. If you're looking for more championship hardware, the brewery was also named Brewpub of the Year by *USA Today* in 2016 and 2017, and the Great American Beer Festival named Titletown the 2015 Large Brewpub of the Year and crowned David Oldenburg Large Brewpub Brewer of the Year in the same year.

The brewing system was located directly behind the bar in this now converted train depot building. It felt good to have this building buzzing with energy once again.

Titletown started as a brewpub, serving food right away. It served a pub-style menu: fish and chips, pot roast and burgers. Weycker wanted to make food that went well with beer—quality food, quality beer. It even had its own in-house bakery dishing up big desserts with elaborately spun sugar.

Going back to Weycker's family history, root beer was brewed right away. Brent's grandmother, Gladys Weycker, was still living at the time Titletown opened. She shared some of her secrets for the root beer profile. He, of course, had to bring back the name Sno Cap Root Beer.

After nearly two decades, Titletown was outgrowing this original space. It expanded across the parking lot to open a new taproom in 2013 inside the old Larson Canning Building. Larson Canning packaged Veg-All, a concoction of canned vegetables. Now Titletown is pouring all of its beer in this street-level taproom, as well as a recent expansion to the Roof Tap in the same building. The rooftop taproom has the best views of the Bay of Green Bay, Fox River and downtown Green Bay.

For the past twenty-five years, Brent was always focused on the operations and hospitality side of the endeavor. He always brought in people who knew much more about beer than he did. This has created a lasting and successful brewery that continues to grow its championship-minded beer.

As a history guy, Brent is also proud to live in Fred Rahr's old home.

HINTERLAND BREWERY

Hinterland—The land beyond. The unexplored. A journey.

Hinterland Brewery is a journey in and of itself and also takes its patrons on their very own journey. This particular journey begins like many other brewers in Green Bay—with a homebrew kit. Bill Tressler received a life-changing Christmas gift from his then girlfriend, now wife, Michelle. He began brewing malt extract beers throughout college at Creighton University. The early beers were admittedly a little hard to get down, but with some tweaking and enjoying the art of beer recipes, Bill started brewing beers that he very much enjoyed drinking.

Bill had a knack for adventure. As a college student at Creighton University in Omaha, Nebraska, he was a literal rock star as the drummer in a band,

Violet Ride. For a college band, they were pretty good, Bill proudly admits. The band eventually moved to San Francisco to begin recording and playing gigs. On weekends, Bill would road trip from Omaha to San Francisco for recording sessions and head back to Creighton for class. Violet Ride was eventually offered a record deal by Monster Records. Unfortunately, the band chose not to sign.

Those classes he was taking were in pursuit of a journalism degree. During their senior year, Bill proposed to Michelle. She said "yes." Neither was sure where they would end up, but both had ideas and dreams of what they wanted to do.

Bill hadn't given up his passion for music, so he began applying to jobs in San Francisco, hoping to be close to his band. Thanks to his excellent journalism degree, the *San Francisco Chronicle* offered Bill a job in May 1993. He and Michelle moved to the West Coast. Bill continued crafting his writing, learning the journalism business and working on his music success. He was still homebrewing out of their little San Francisco apartment. He had rigged up an elaborate system, taking up half of the apartment space.

There was a looming journalist strike at the *San Francisco Chronicle*. While overcoming these speed bumps, Bill eventually caught a huge break. He met Bill Owens. Bill was an owner of one of the first brewpubs in the country, Buffalo Bill's. As if Bill Owens had not done enough pioneering by opening the brewpub, Buffalo Bill's pumpkin ale is one of the first, if not the very first, pumpkin ales brewed in the modern brewing era. He was also an owner of Owens Publishing, which oversaw *American Brewer Magazine* and *Beer: The Magazine*. Bill Owens offered Bill Tressler a job as editor of *Beer: The Magazine*.

This new job allowed Tressler to learn more about beer, and he realized he still had a long way to go. So far that he enrolled in the fermentation science and engineering program at University of California, Davis. On finishing the program at UC Davis, Bill got internships at Niagara Falls Brewing Company and Wynkoop Brewery. The latter was in preparation for the opening of Green Bay's Titletown Brewing Company.

Bill and Michelle decided to move back to their hometown of Green Bay after spending just two years in California. Titletown Brewing had approached Bill to bring his brewing knowledge to its project. After some investment negotiation conversations, Bill decided that he and Michelle would try their go at opening their own place.

They leased a former cheese factory building in Denmark, Wisconsin. They never intended to be so far out of Green Bay, but the price and space were right for a start-up brewery. Hinterland's Green Bay Brewing Company began brewing in May 1995. Michelle did all of the bookkeeping, marketing and sales. Bill did all of the brewing and production.

Cock & Bull Publick House was the first bar to pour Hinterland beer on November 9, 1995. Two beers were on tap: a pale ale and an amber. Neither of these is made anymore. From the very early days, Bill made a decision to continually update beers to stay relevant. He had seen too many breweries and beers decline because they refused to try new things. Hinterland would not be such a place.

In May 1998, Hinterland moved its operations to the old Spence Corporation building on Dousman Street in downtown Green Bay. Tressler added a fireplace room with a bit of a Northwoods cabin feel to it, featuring brick walls, a large chandelier and a cozy atmosphere. There was a taproom for socializing. The bottling line came right out into the taproom. Initially, there was no food served with the exception of a charcuterie platter.

The taproom on the corner of Dousman and Broadway opened in the summer of 1999. The beer was flowing, and people were imbibing. Not only was the beer a major success but the space also brought an influx of inquiries to rent the taproom to host private parties. It got to a point where there was one or two every week.

This was a major factor in the decision to add a full commercial restaurant kitchen. Tressler had always considered himself a foodie. He cut his teeth in San Francisco and Denver—two cities on the successfully trendy and creative side of beer and cuisine. Bill brought these West Coast food ideas and culture to Green Bay.

Approaching the decade mark in this downtown location, Hinterland had outgrown the space. Bill used some creative maneuvering to cram something productive into every last nook and cranny of this building.

As they say, timing is everything. Bill got a phone call in 2012. The Green Bay Packers were on the other end. Bill already had a relationship with them. Executives would often entertain guests at Hinterland over dinner and some beers. Tressler also had a conversation with them during the first stadium expansion about the possibility of opening a brewpub at Lambeau Field. That didn't work out, but Bill was about to be offered an even sweeter opportunity.

That phone call was about an entertainment district that was being planned west of Lambeau Field. The team would like Bill to explore this opportunity. Bill saw a map of the entire area. The conversation quickly went to having Hinterland on the corner of Lombardi Avenue and Ridge Road—literally across the street from Lambeau Field. This was a dream come true. The goal was to have Hinterland as one of the anchors to the Titletown District.

Bill's response was one of obvious and immediate excitement; however, Hinterland needed to expand right then. With his excitement and optimism, Bill trusted in the process with the assurance that these things have a way of working themselves out. And they did. Tressler signed a nondisclosure agreement and an eventual letter of intent to move his Hinterland operation right across from 1265 Lombardi Avenue.

In 2016, Bill stood at the future spot of his new location to put a ceremonial shovel into the ground, announcing Hinterland as an anchor to Titletown District. A year later, in March 2017, Hinterland opened its new doors with breathtaking views of Lambeau Field and still serving the highest-quality beer and food.

The Hinterland journey still feels too good to be true for Bill. Every morning, he walks through the doors wondering how he got so lucky. He often hears the voice in his head, with a childlike excitement, reminding him, "I can't believe I work here."

"Every beer is created by [brewmaster] Joe Karls, Bill and the whole Hinterland Brewery crew. They each contain backstories of brew trials, recipe tweaks and many tales of late-night tastings....From somewhat traditional beers and popular pilsners to downright decadently weird renditions of specialty brews, Hinterland can take your tasting tour to a dark place pretty fast. That's the beauty of Hinterland—we can push your comfort zone with a gentle nudge or club it over the head with a totally new, mind-blowing experience."

That is Hinterland. Enjoy the journey.

STILLMANK BREWING COMPANY

*College kid drinks a lot of beer. College kid homebrews beer.
Now a professional brewer.*

A college kid from Wisconsin heads west for school and ends up drinking a lot of beer. Details may differ, but there's probably many who can relate to at least the latter half of the story. That may be as far as the parallels go.

Brad Stillmank attended Fort Lewis College in Durango, Colorado, to pursue a marketing degree. Durango is a high-elevation—seven thousand feet above sea level—desert town with a population of fifteen thousand people. The closest city is Albuquerque, New Mexico, almost four hours away.

Brad worked hard and partied even harder. His go-to beer was Schaefer and plenty of it. He chose this by default because he could get a twelve-pack for five dollars. This was plenty suitable drinking for a broke college student. His friends were starting to expand their tastes (and their beer budget) to higher-end craft beer bombers. These twenty-two-ounce bottles were often more expensive than Brad's entire twelve-pack.

Rather than continuing to watch his friends drink these high-quality beers and wishing he could join them, he decided he would just make his own. His first homebrew was a red ale kit. His recollection of it was that everyone really liked it. That's what kept him brewing his own beer—one after another. In hindsight, and most likely reality, it was probably terrible beer, but his friends appreciated the free beer, so they said nice things about it. Regardless, Brad kept brewing and continued perfecting his process and recipes until he actually was making the high-quality beer his friends had been paying premium dollar for.

After he graduated with a bachelor's degree in business marketing in 2001, Brad's grandma asked him what his plan was now. He told her about his passion for this homebrewing hobby he had picked up. He could see making beer an even bigger part of his life than it already was. Her advice may have cemented Brad's future as a brewer. She told him if that was what he really wanted to do, then he should get formal training to be his best at it. If Brad could find a school where he could receive a brewer's education to make a legitimate career out of it, she would put up half of the tuition dollars.

University of California, Davis had an online certification program in brewing and packaging. Brad was accepted into the program. At the same time, he landed a job with Ska Brewing in Durango as a packaging guy—he washed kegs and filled bottles. On completing his brewing and packaging certifications from UC Davis in 2004, Brad was able to work his way into the cellar at Ska Brewing. This eventually led to writing beer recipes for the brewery. He ultimately became one of the lead brewers there.

As Brad puts it, "Durango had six breweries kicking ass in a town the size of Allouez [Wisconsin]." The beer environment out there was unique and booming. He would go to a brewpub for breakfast because it was also a bakery. While the average person has toast and coffee, Brad would order a donut and a raspberry beer for breakfast. That was just the life out there at the time for Brad—not a bad one, either, he would add.

Brad Stillmank homebrewing before Stillmank Brewing Company existed. He learned the brewing craft while living in Colorado and brought his dream back to his home state. *Photo courtesy of Brad Stillmank.*

Life in Colorado was expensive. Brad, his girlfriend at the time, now wife, Erin, and another friend in the brewing industry owned a house together so they could all afford it. The house was located about half an hour from Durango in Bayfield, a small town of about five hundred residents. They had an acre of land and dogs running around, and whether at work or at home, life was a nonstop party. By all accounts, times were fun, and life was good.

Erin and Brad were about to get married, though. The two of them were trying to figure out what their future life together was going to look like. Erin was wanting to go back to school to further her nursing career. There were some West Coast schools with good programs that were on the radar until Bellin College in Green Bay popped up on Erin's list of potential schools. Bellin College was a quality school with a quicker program than most of the others Erin was considering. Brad was looking forward to the opportunity to move back to his home state.

When they got to Green Bay in 2007, they saw that Brown County, a community of 250,000 people, only had two breweries. They had just left a town that was a fraction of the size that had three times as many thriving breweries. The beer was good in Green Bay, but there were more than enough people to support another.

Brad now saw his mission in Green Bay while Erin was going to school full time. The ultimate goal was to open a brewery, but the two needed to make some money first. Kay Distributing hired Brad to sell and distribute beers.

Taking his beer skills and knowledge to the next level, Brad became one of the first certified cicerones in the country. According to the Cicerone Certification Program website, Stillmank is still one of only two who hold this title in Green Bay. A cicerone is to beer what a sommelier is to wine. Certified cicerone is the second level for beer professionals dedicated to quality beer. This course provides advanced knowledge in storing and serving beer, beer flavor and evaluation expertise, beer ingredients and brewing process mastery and beer pairings skills.

In 2011, Stillmank finally had enough money saved up to buy forty-eight empty half-barrel kegs. Leftover money was used to buy a couple batches of grain. Thanks to his eight years with Kay Distributing, Brad had developed relationships with brewers all over Wisconsin.

Milwaukee Brewing Company had just purchased a new brewing warehouse after outgrowing its brewpub. It now had this brand-new, huge production facility that it hadn't quite grown into. It was purchased with the anticipation of major growth. Brad knew there was plenty of room for an idea.

He needed a facility to help him get his brewing business started. Brad would ship his kegs to Milwaukee Brewing, pay for all the ingredients, rent some space and use the equipment to brew his own beer. Brad was also excited Milwaukee had a canning line. Canning is what almost all breweries in Colorado were doing. He was more than comfortable serving his beer in cans.

Brad and Milwaukee Brewing Company worked up a five-year contract so that he could use their facility to brew his own beer. The state officially recognizes this relationship as a recipe brewer; it is colloquially known as contract brewing.

Stillmank's beer was branded as Wisco Disco, an extra special bitter (ESB). Explaining it as such was not easily marketable around Green Bay. Comparing it to a hoppy amber turned out to be much more successful.

As with any good name comes a good story. Brad's buddy Spencer came up with it. Spencer and Brad worked at Kay Distributing together. On a sales call one day, the two beer guys started talking about what it would be like to open a bar. Spencer noticed how Wisconsin bars have unique feels and specific characteristics to them. Generally, there's Packers memorabilia all over the inside, pickled eggs behind the bar and Old Fashioneds being poured. The conversation turned to how cool it would be to open these niche bars all over the country, bringing a bit of Wisconsin to everyone. Spencer suggested that they would call them Wisco Disco.

Two years later, the Wisco Disco bar hadn't panned out, so the next best thing was to have a beer named for it. All of the Wisco Disco beer was brewed in Milwaukee but brought back to sell in Green Bay. Kay Distributing served as Stillmank's distributor throughout the Green Bay area.

Nicky's in De Pere was the first establishment to tap Stillmank's Wisco Disco. There was a kick-off party in May 2012 at Nicky's, pouring the first keg for eagerly waiting beer drinkers. That first year, about a dozen other bars picked up Wisco Disco. Stillmank had no retail or taproom sales. It was just a few bars buying into this beer and hoping their customers would drink it. And drink it they did.

After building a base of Wisco Disco drinkers, Brad used Milwaukee Brewing Company's canning line. Brad and Kay Distribution got Wisco Disco on the shelves in some local grocery and liquor stores to reach a whole new market.

This scenario played out for two years. During this entire time, Brad was pitching banks for a loan to start building his own physical brewery in Green Bay. There was a small problem. Brad was barely breaking even with his current setup at the Milwaukee Brewing Company. But he saw the positives in just doing what he had to do to build his brand and establish a loyal following of those who wanted to drink Stillmank beer.

In April 2014, all the hard work finally paid off—literally. Stillmank received a loan to purchase an old warehouse in downtown Green Bay's east side. The building was owned by Builders Supply Company.

Brad had looked at dozens of possible buildings and locations to find the ideal space to build a brewery and taproom. This warehouse had high ceilings with plenty of open floor space. It also came at the right price. These were the perfect ingredients for Stillmank Brewing Company to make something of its own.

Builders Supply had sold most of its other buildings in the area, but this one had been vacant for years. It was commercially zoned but had zero parking spaces for employees, which is a violation of building codes. The parking situation worked when the area was all owned by the same company, allowing employees to park in a variety of lots, but as properties were split up and sold, this changed.

Stillmank actually removed a portion of the building to create a much-needed parking lot. To make this a whole family affair, Brad's recently retired father offered to be the general contractor to transform the space to meet his son's vision.

With construction on a remodel underway, Brad continued to brew in Milwaukee to keep building the Stillmank brand. In July 2014, the state and national brewing licenses were transferred to Green Bay, officially making this Henry Street location a brewery. The Stillmank Brewing Company operation commenced.

During the short transition from brewing in Milwaukee to Green Bay, bars quickly depleted their Wisco Disco inventory—an optimistic problem in Brad's eyes. He quickly got Wisco Disco back up and running in his new facility.

Once the bars were happily restocked, Brad dug down to his roots in the beer industry with new recipe writing so that he could begin brewing a variety of beers. Ahead of a grand opening, Stillmank knew he would need more beers offered in the taproom.

Brad went from an employee of Kay Distributing to a full-time supplier to Kay when Stillmank opened its doors in October 2014. Even with a taproom, distribution was (and still is) the major focus for Stillmank Brewing.

On opening the taproom, Stillmank had three beers on tap: Wisco Disco, Super Kind IPA and Bee's Knees Honey Rye. The honey rye style did not work out as well as Brad was expecting. With doubt in his mind about whether he had made the right decision and a whole lot of Bee's Knees in inventory to sell, he had to figure out a way to get people to enjoy it. The creative side of Brad's brewer mind jumped at the opportunity to problem solve.

He installed a HopRocket on the Bee's Knees tap line. A HopRocket is a contraption connected to the tap line where beer passes through a product for extra flavor on its way to the faucet. Often, a HopRocket is filled with, of course, fresh hops. This is where Brad's creativity and passion for beer came to life. Brad ran Bee's Knees through a HopRocket filled with fresh jalapeños. He called this variation Killer Bees. Killer Bees may have just been a novelty to get people to try it. Once they did, though, they loved it. The kegs full of Bees were flying off the inventory shelves. The key was just a little spice and a good story about hot peppers in a HopRocket.

Another successful Stillmank HopRocket venture was pouring the Perky Porter, brewed with locally roasted La Java coffee, through freshly roasted coffee beans. This created the Double Perky Porter. Order a Perky Porter in the taproom, and you'll get a donut hole on the side.

Five years in, Stillmank is still reliant on bars selling more beers than his taproom. The taproom is really a marketing piece for the beer. Brad knows that when the bars succeed, he succeeds, and when he succeeds, the bars succeed. It's a mutually supportive relationship.

The taproom has a neighborhood bar feel to it. Brad attributes this to his days at Ska Brewing. It was the kind of setting where people would get off work and stop in the taproom for one pint and a conversation before taking a growler home. This neighborly community mindset is evident at Stillmank with its buy-a-friend-a-beer program. Pay in advance for a beer, put your friend's name on the board and the next time your buddy walks in, he or she will have a beer waiting.

The next time you're at Stillmank looking to put someone's name on the board, remember me, Cameron Teske.

Stillmank's focus was to create beers you could drink more than one of, typically referred to as session beers. This can be tough in the craft beer industry, especially as of late, when many brewers are going for shock value or the next niche beer. While that's fun, Brad's trying to sell pallets of beer while continuing to deliver quality.

In 2020, Brad is brewing about two thousand barrels per year. His buisness has been growing at about 15 percent per year for five years. He knows it's almost time for an expansion for continued growth, and that is, no doubt, the whole goal.

Badger State Brewing Company

Wisconsinite: To be a Badger and drink beer.

It was the summer of 2012 when childhood friends Andrew Fabry and Mike Servi spent an afternoon brewing beer with Mike's cousin Sam Yanda. Their first brew was an autumn ale that would be ready to drink as fall approached.

Throughout the summer, their brewing hobby quickly took up much of their free time. They were writing recipes, piecing together bigger and bigger homebrewing systems and making it a fun social setting for the three friends to spend time together. All three guys grew up in Green Bay, hanging out, playing sports and beaming with Wisconsin pride. Each of them brings a unique aspect to the group and the brewery.

Andrew hopped around colleges a bit—from Arizona to North Dakota and finally graduating with a psychology degree from University of Wisconsin–Madison. Yes, he is a Badger.

Mike attended University of Wisconsin–Eau Claire to pursue a career in environmental science. He did a stint with the Wisconsin Department of Natural Resources but quickly realized this wasn't for him and began applying to optometry programs around the country.

Sam received a degree in finance from University of Wisconsin–Platteville. His banking jobs in the real world just weren't as fulfilling as he would have liked.

All three are products of the University of Wisconsin system. All three are Badgers at heart.

Andrew, Mike and Sam were in Green Bay during the summer of 2012, when they discovered their new hobby of homebrewing. Andrew was a recent graduate with no steady career. Sam was unhappy with his job. Mike was in the process of a major life transition.

Hanging out in a pool drinking beers, the conversation went from casually chatting about their current beer obsession to the real possibility of turning their homebrewing summer activity into something more.

Shortly after that day in the pool, Andrew went to work drafting a business plan. He did market research and found that there were no production-only breweries in town—only brewpub restaurants. This would be their niche. This would get back to the core of what brewing in Green Bay had historically been.

Mere months after the first homebrew session, Badger State Brewing incorporated in February 2013. While the business plan was being written, they also continued brewing beer on almost a weekly basis. They were working to perfect their craft and grow their inventory.

Andrew and his crew wanted to bring the craft of craft beer to Green Bay. Their beers would be layered with complexity—still very drinkable but with plenty of character. The Bunyan Badger Brown Ale includes rye malt that is not usually seen in such a style of beer. This brings an unusual spice or umami note. Green Chop IPA was designed to be a session India Pale Ale—not too hoppy and lower in alcohol by volume than standard IPAs. At the time this recipe was written, IPAs were trying to out hop one another, but Badger State wanted an approachable and drinkable one. On Wisconsin! Red Ale took the opposite approach when the team upped the ABV and added some hoppiness not often found in a traditional red ale.

No matter what kind of beer they brewed, they stuck to their morals to make the purest beer they could. Each beer they made had to receive their high-quality stamp of approval. There would be no off flavors or tang to their beer. Early in their business of brewing beer, a friend offered Andrew insight that has stuck with him ever since: "You can either be a brewery who dumps beer or a brewery who serves anything they make. Which brewery are you going to be?" This mindset ensures quality, even at the cost of losing product not up to standards. (Badger State has had to dump fewer batches than they can count on one hand, but they know they're willing to if the brew just doesn't stand up to their standards.)

Each person's palate is different. Having three guys try a beer will bring different results. It was a fun process to learn one another's tastes and how they would each react to the same beer. Andrew, Mike and Sam enjoyed comparing their own experience with each beer and tweaking the recipes until they were just right.

Badger State Brewing moved its operation into a small part of an old warehouse in the summer of 2013. To be specific, it was the old locker room in the warehouse. The space wasn't big, but it fit what they needed at the time.

There were a few hotels near this location, and it was down the road from Lambeau Field and the Resch Center. They also knew in the back of their minds that a brewery had the potential to be the cornerstone of a neighborhood redevelopment. This was their optimistic hope of this relatively vacant area of Green Bay.

Sam left his job in October 2013, which was a leap of faith. To make this successful, he knew he had to focus on brewing full time. They still didn't have an opening date in mind. They were creating inventory and turning their small space into something of a makeshift taproom—one that didn't actually serve beer for consumption on premises.

There still wasn't a detailed plan to open, but they decided at the last second there is no time like the present. That was a Thursday. They posted on Facebook that the next day, December 6, 2013, Badger State Brewing would be open and selling growlers of beer from the facility on Tony Canadeo Run.

They had no idea how many people would show up, if any. The *Green Bay Press Gazette* crime beat reporter was the first customer. Then more showed up. People continued to come through the doors to get beer to take home. To keep up with demand, the brewers held a rigorous, around-the-clock brewing schedule. If the door was locked, customers would knowingly and continuously ring the doorbell until they got their beer. People wanted Badger State beer, and that felt really good for some recent college graduates looking to find their path in life.

This process continued for a while. Badger State had its regular customers and often welcomed brand-new ones as well. Some would order their beer and leave right away. But many would stay and chat with the guys. Andrew and Sam were happy to talk beer with their customers. The whole brewing process started for these guys to be social and spend time together. Being social and spending time with those who enjoy drinking their beer was absolutely no different.

But something was missing.

The next spring, they began making plans to have an actual taproom, where they could enjoy a freshly poured pint with their loyal beer drinkers. This entailed moving to another part of the warehouse building. They did a lot of the work themselves. Again, while continuing to brew beer.

The taproom opened less than a year after they started their growler gig. If it worked once, it could work twice—another Facebook post promoted this opening. So many people showed up that the taproom was packed. Badger State Brewing was blown away.

This entire time, they were still brewing on their original one-barrel, souped-up homebrew system. It was time to expand to a professional fifteen-barrel system. They hired a buddy of Sam's who had been involved with some larger successful breweries to help with the transition of learning a new, much larger operation.

Recipe scaling was not as simple as expected. This is where science and creativity meet to ensure the same quality product Badger State drinkers have loved since day one can come out of a brand-new process.

Badger State's success has continued to grow. The team brewed 175 barrels of beer in the first year. In 2018, they brewed 2,000 barrels. In 2019, they transitioned, yet again, to a thirty-barrel system. Badger State has a vision to continue growing while brewing the favorite beers that got them to where they are today.

The taproom boasts an impressive twenty beers on tap. Many of the taps pour rotating Badger State beers, but they also welcome guest beers made in Wisconsin. Badger State Brewing's staple beers include Green Chop Session IPA, Bunyan Badger Brown Ale, On Wisconsin! Red Ale, Walloon Witbier, Buzzy Badger Coffee Ale and Peninsula Pils Craft Lager.

Green Chop Session IPA: Farming is hard, all-day work, and in Wisconsin, it's a way of life. Badger State celebrates the bountiful work of farmers by blending six different American hop varieties for a less-bitter, easy-drinking, session IPA with light, bright, fresh flavor.

Bunyan Badger Brown Ale: This brown ale is full of big, bold character, hence the name from one of the most popular tall tales and an animal with determination.

On Wisconsin! Red Ale: This is a classic American amber with a Badger State spin. It's brewed with Wisconsin malt and all-American hops with a hint of light orange zest. The label proudly displays the Wisconsin state motto: "Forward."

Walloon Witbier: This Belgian-style witbier pays homage to some of the early European immigrants to northeast Wisconsin. Walloon Witbier is crisp and clean with a unique mix of tart fruit and fresh spice flavors.

Buzzy Badger Coffee Ale: If you're like the Badger State guys, the best way to start your day is with a hot cup of coffee, and the best way to end your day is with a cold pint of beer. This beer drinks like a cold-brew coffee and throws havoc to the age-old question: Coffee or beer?

Peninsula Pils Craft Lager: Green Bay sits at the base of the Door County Peninsula. The golden suds of this lager reflect the golden sun on a warm summer day and the sparkling waters of the Bay of Green Bay.

The classic lager-style beer helped build Wisconsin into the beer state that it is. BRWSKI dug to the roots of the classic German-inspired brew. As an added bonus, the can is a vanity Wisconsin license plate. *Photo courtesy of Badger State Brewing Company.*

An addition of a seven-barrel pilot system in 2019 also gave the team an opportunity to experiment and have some fun coming up with the next favorite beers to be poured in the taproom. The larger pilot batches allow for more feedback and the ability to develop and discuss beers as they age over a few weeks. This also brings in some fun of an expanded barrel-aging program. Badger State fans are looking forward to drinking beer art in a Badger State pint glass.

From their perspective, they're only getting started. Forward.

NOBLE ROOTS BREWING COMPANY

Family bonding rooted in beer.

In 2007, Tyler Falish went on a study abroad stint in Utrecht, Netherlands. His family came to visit him and learn about his new favorite European hangouts. While exploring, their palates were opened to quality European beers. Prior to this, they mostly preferred domestic lights. They all returned to the United States with a new appreciation for beer.

The Falish family—father Marvin, son Tyler and son Alex—took a try at homebrewing and replicating some of the beers they learned to love in Europe. During the early days, Alex was a little young to be able to enjoy the final product, but he still learned plenty and would help how he could.

Initially the brew system was a five-gallon process on Mom's stovetop. This worked well for a while, until one day it didn't. During the brewing process of a Belgian Trippel, one of the Falish boys turned his back on the brew at just the wrong time. The sticky extract boiled over onto Mom's brand-new glass stovetop. The kitchen was instantly filled with smoke, and the whole house smelled of burnt wort.

While feeling bad about making a disaster in the kitchen, the boys were told to buy whatever equipment they needed to set up their brewing operation in the garage and out of her kitchen. It all worked out.

Now in the garage, Marv, Tyler and Alex began brewing constantly. Each brew welcomed over a dozen other family members, friends and neighbors to hang out while the beer was being made. Some would put in their two cents here and there, but many were there just to enjoy the previous batch's final product.

Jordan Sullivan and Tyler, Alex and Marv Falish homebrewing out of their garage while enjoying some of their previous brew. *Photo courtesy of Noble Roots Brewing Company.*

Garage doors are open on a beautiful fall day in Green Bay for some fresh air in the Noble Roots Brewing Company taproom. *Photo courtesy of Noble Roots Brewing Company.*

It came to a point when they literally couldn't keep up with the drinking. They were getting about forty-eight bottles out of each batch. Family and friends couldn't get enough of this homebrew. Five years after beginning this beer endeavor, it was time to upgrade yet again.

Downtown Green Bay's House of Homebrew store had a fifteen-gallon all-grain system on sale. This took a step from hobby homebrewing to pretty advanced brewing that just happened to be operated out of their garage. The first beer to come out of this half-barrel system was a double IPA.

Taking this brewing hobby to a new level, Marv, Alex and Jordan Sullivan (who married into the family) joined the Green Bay Rackers, a local homebrew club. It was a great opportunity for Marv and company to learn from talented homebrewers in the Green Bay area and to officially become part of this burgeoning beer community.

While this homebrewing operation grew, Alex was attending the University of Wisconsin–Madison, his older brother's alma mater. Continuing to hone his brewing skills, Alex spent his long walks across campus listening to brewing podcasts. Aside from pursuing his degree, he read books on brewing. He picked up anything he could get his hands on that advanced his knowledge on the science of beer.

As the homebrewing process expanded from a mere hobby to a borderline obsession, it seemed they had all the technical knowledge and the right personnel involved to seriously contemplate taking this from a family pastime to a professional endeavor. They planned this while hanging out in Marv's pool during the summer of 2014.

The full cast of characters consisted of the patriarch, Marv Falish, sons Tyler and Alex Falish and Marv's son-in-law Jordan Sullivan. Each of their professional backgrounds offered some serious assets that would allow this dream to become a successful reality. Marv previously worked for a beer distributor. Tyler held a strategic marketing job. Alex knew shipping and logistics. Jordan brought financial expertise. As the conversation progressed, these guys became excited to begin pursuing something bigger as a very real possibility.

Being a member of the Green Bay Rackers brought invaluable advice. Their relationships with some of the area brewers also gave them a community to ask questions and learn from any mistakes these brewers were willing to share.

January 2015 was an exciting month that got them closer toward the finish line of opening a brewery. They found a building on Washington Street in downtown Green Bay that would be an ideal location for opening the small brewing operation they envisioned. The building offered two stories of brewing space, with a third floor of already occupied offices. They hired an architect to begin drawing out their dream. However, as a small endeavor, they were trying to save money any way they could. After work one day, Marv and Alex raced over to the building to begin measuring the entire space before it got dark. They had nothing more than a tape measure.

After spending eight months of working out the details of this two-story brewery, the architect came across something that left him feeling uneasy. This was an older building. They were planning to bring in a lot of heating equipment, which comes with the territory of brewing beer. Rather than just being required to install fire prevention sprinklers in their space, the entire building would have to be outfitted with sprinklers. On a leased building, this just did not seem like a viable or wise option. They had to walk away from this building.

Devastated and feeling like they just wasted nearly a year, they didn't lose hope that things would work out. One fall afternoon, Marv was driving around for work and passed a small unoccupied building on Green Bay's east side along University Avenue. He texted Alex the address.

Alex pulled property records in minutes and immediately shot down Marv's idea. The building was too small and not laid out to handle a brewing operation. Marv still thought it could work but didn't fight Alex on it. Alex showed up to Marv's house four hours after that text conversation. Based on the footprint of the building and some rough measurements, Alex rethought this option. He brought an entire hand-drawn plan, showing this was not only a real possibility but also a really good option.

Through this entire project, they had to learn many new things as they went. There are parallels between that mindset and homebrewing. With a mentality like that, they knew they were cut out for this and would somehow make it work.

The fun part was that the building wasn't even for sale. They had to find the owner and convince him to sell. Oh, and while trying to convince him, they also needed to jump through hoops and over hurdles to get the appropriate permits and zoning requirements to open a brewery in this building. Historically, the building had opened as a Sinclair gas station in 1967. Throughout the rest of its existence, it was a showroom for fireplaces, a mechanic shop, an IT facility, a scuba shop and a window tinting and car detailing garage. The Falish family anticipated adding brewery and taproom to that dossier.

The building was located in Schmitt Park, an established neighborhood. One of the major hurdles, and arguably the most important, to overcome was earning the support of the homeowners in the area. This quiet neighborhood was less than excited to hear that a tavern was moving in. "Tavern" was the official category of this zoning application.

Marvin, Alex and Jordan put on their best public relations hats and went to work introducing themselves to their future neighbors. They attended neighborhood association meetings to share their vision for this brewery taproom and to clarify the difference between this and a standard bar. The public raised many valid concerns about a facility serving intoxicants. However, at the end of the day, Marv, Alex and Jordan did a great job explaining the craft beer crowd to these concerned neighbors. These types of patrons walk through the door looking for quality rather than quantity.

They eventually received the keys to the building in May 2016. Work began immediately on a renovation and remodel to turn this mechanic building to a brewery. Dumpster after dumpster worth of trash went out the door. Family and friends pitched in anywhere they could bring their skill set. This family-inspired project was completed at the hard work of just such people, family—by relation and by choice.

Jordan Sullivan and Alex and Marv Falish hang the first Noble Roots Brewing Company sign at the future home of the brewery after purchasing the vacant building. *Photo courtesy of Noble Roots Brewing Company.*

While the building was being worked on, the Falish family was going through the federal application process to receive their brewer's license. They officially filed as Noble Roots Brewing Company.

The beer was always a family affair, so the name had to reflect that. Marv passed a magnificent tree with beautifully exposed roots on his road trips to Madison while his children were going to school there. It caught his attention every time he passed it. Throughout this process, that tree kept popping into his head. Eventually, the conversation gravitated toward a family tree with deep roots. Showing of high character and fine qualities is what they wanted their beer to be: Noble. Noble Roots Brewing Company was established.

After finally getting the feds' approval in December 2016, they quickly went to work to start brewing a quality product that would impress their new patrons. Six beers were ready to pour at Noble Roots Brewing Company's grand opening on March 3, 2017.

At the grand opening, Noble Roots poured six beers they were incredibly proud of:

Mackinac Island Amber: This was the first batch they brewed in their new brewery. During their homebrewing days, an original rendition of this beer was created for a road trip to Mackinac Island, Michigan, with Tyler and a bunch of buddies.

Hapsburg Pretender: This easy sipping American blonde ale plays a great pilsner imposter but is brewed right here in Green Bay and not in Pilsen, Czech Republic.

Noble Roots IPA: The flagship IPA is a refreshing citrus ale.

Blonde Belgian: Marv Fallish is 100 percent Belgian. This brew is the epitome of the hard work, Belgian blood, sweat and tears that went into opening this brewery.

Cardinal IPA: This third coast IPA has a malty sweetness and a caramel reddish color.

Midnight Confection: This chocolate stout is midnight dark and full of chocolatey confections.

Noble Roots began as and continues to be a self-distributing brewery. With Marv's experience in distribution and Alex's logistics knowledge, they have mastered this simple way to keep their own revenue. The only thing limiting their distribution is whether they have enough of the beer in stock that a bar is requesting and the number of tanks in the building.

Marv and Alex Falish displaying their Noble Roots Brewing Company wear at an outdoor festival. *Photo courtesy of Noble Roots Brewing Company.*

For the first year and a half, the entire operation was run by family. Now, they have expanded to hiring others—just to pour the beer though. It still is and always will be Falish-brewed beer.

COPPER STATE BREWING COMPANY

A mechanical engineer walks into a brewery…

No, that's not the start of a nerdy joke. That was the beginning of Copper State Brewing Company. Before we dive too far into Copper State, let's back up a bit.

As Hinterland Brewery was working through a deal to move its operation to the new Titletown District near Lambeau Field, a trusted realtor was secretly shopping its building located on the corner of Dousman Street and Broadway in downtown Green Bay.

This realtor reached out to Bill Heiges of Appleton's Copper Rock Coffee Shop. Heiges knew he wanted this building as he was receiving the tour and sales pitch. The catch was that a coffee shop couldn't survive here alone. The space was just too big. It was also being sold with all of Hinterland's old brewing equipment and full-service kitchen space.

Heiges reached out to his sister-in-law and brother-in-law, Missy and Jon Martens, to see if they would be interested in joining this potential brewery venture. Missy and Jon were living in Saint Paul, Minnesota. Jon had never brewed a batch of beer in his life. But Missy and Jon had a surprisingly difficult decision to make: should they move their four kids three hundred miles to pursue this exciting opportunity of which they knew nothing about and of which they could not yet speak a word to anyone? Hinterland's move was still a very delicate secret.

Jon was stuck in a stagnant engineering job, dealing with heating and cooling systems. He's a problem solver and a creative thinker. Complacency goes against every part of his being. He was born in Puerto Rico while his father was a missionary. As is often the case with a missionary lifestyle, Jon and his family moved a lot growing up. Jon is used to new things and welcomes the unknown.

The science-minded part of Jon knew that he could intellectually brew beer. The creative-minded part of Jon was excited to throw some ingredients together to make an end product people loved to drink.

Jon and Missy sat on their almost-finished back patio in Minnesota one night, having a conversation about what to do, both knowing they'd finish the patio project just in time to sell the house and move to Green Bay.

Jon and Missy, Bill and Em Heiges, Gregg and Heather Mattek and a few other partners purchased the Hinterland building in October 2015. Hinterland rented it back until they were officially ready to move to their new location. Missy and Jon were still living in the Twin Cities, quietly creating a plan to run and operate a brewery and restaurant.

Jon continued full time at his engineering day job, while moonlighting at home secretly planning this new brewing adventure. After officially purchasing a brewery, Jon thought it wise to begin homebrewing to get a feel for what he had gotten himself into. Batch after batch was drinkable, but he never *loved* what he was making.

While he never considered himself a beer connoisseur, he had a good enough palate to dissect the brew. He relied on his engineering experience to know how and what to tweak slightly to eventually master his product and get the result he wanted. After several attempts, what would eventually become One Cent Wheat was poured for some friends. Their reaction was a revelation that gave him the satisfaction of a seasoned brewmaster. He was now ready to take on this endeavor with confidence.

Part of the nighttime planning included naming the brewery. Several names were suggested, and some of the suggested names were used later in the beer names. Copper State Brewing Company was the decision. The Green Bay area up through Oconto and into Michigan's Upper Peninsula was called the Old Copper Complex. There was plenty of copper to be found in northeast Wisconsin. The logo, consisting of a copper mosaic hop design creating the state of Wisconsin, even calls attention to the hard work that went into the copper harvesting business. It was a great parallel to the hard work of creating this new brewing company.

The name also went well with Copper Rock Coffee, named for the Copper Mountain Range out west, which Bill Heiges enjoyed skiing. The coffee company even had a mountain as its logo. Synergy between the names made sense.

As part of the agreement to purchase the building, Jon, Missy and company would be flexible on Hinterland's move-out date if Hinterland agreed to take Jon under its wing and offer him an apprenticeship. Jon moved to Green Bay in July 2016 to study under Hinterland's brewmaster, Joe Karls. Jon also spent a six-week stint at Siebel Institute of Technology (SIT) in Chicago. SIT has focused on brewing education and brewing services since 1868.

Copper State Brewing Company officially took over the brewery after Hinterland moved out on April 1, 2017. Jon immediately got to work brewing beer. Six batches went into production before beginning a quick renovation project to make the building their own.

The first six beers brewed out of Copper State Brewing Company were:

One Cent Wheat: This was named after the copper wheat penny, worth exactly one cent. It was also a nod to the copper complex from which their name derived.

Bare Brick IPA: Named as an ode to the beautifully exposed bare brick walls in this old building.

Kupfur Kölsch: A German Kölsh-style beer. *Kupfur* means "copper" in German.

Northwestern Alt: This malt-forward, bready beer is named after a pastoral school that many of the owners had ties to. There are plenty of almost-pastors and pastors' kids in the group.

Silent Canary Double IPA: Although the copper found, not mined, in northeast Wisconsin is known as float copper, the name of this beer is a loose play on the process of mining. Canaries were used to determine if the air in mines was safe to breathe. Just as the natural gas in a mine can sneak up on you, so does this smooth-drinking beer's ABV, sitting at a cool 8.2 percent. Copper State also has a tongue-in-cheek policy for this beer: it's not suitable to be served to miners. For the record, they realize none of their beers are to be served to minors, either.

Platinum Blonde Coffee Stout: Copper State, no doubt, uses Copper Rock Coffee whenever it can. The unique twist on this stout is that it is a golden blonde.

As these beers brewed, the team went to work renovating the space to create an all-in-one brewpub, taproom and coffee shop space.

The building was originally built in 1919 as the Swift Meat Packing Plant. The old freight elevator in Copper State's taproom is original to the building. Above the bar, you can still see the holes in the ceiling where slabs of meat would hang throughout the mid-twentieth century. Throughout the entire space, you'll see plenty of repurposed bricks. Many of them are charred. These bricks most likely came from Swift's meat smoke room. Swift Meat Packing moved out in the late 1960s or early 1970s. Hinterland moved in during the mid-1990s and got it prepared to be a restaurant and brewery.

Copper State's renovation was a quick two-month turnaround in preparation to open its doors on June 1, 2017. With six beers on tap and a fully prepared food menu, Copper State was off to a great start in a community thriving with craft beer.

This would never have been possible without some very important players. Missy and Jon are not the only owners and influencers. Missy does all of the marketing and witty writing of the beer descriptors and the website, and she has embodied the persona of the High Brau Frau in the Copper State blog. Jon's cousin Gregg Mattek and his wife, Heather, are part owners, as well. Gregg works for Google but enjoys this side project as a nice creative outlet. Heather can often be found hosting or serving as barista. Em and Bill are mostly at their Appleton location of Copper Rock Coffee. Bill makes the trek to Green Bay at least once a week to roast coffee beans.

Copper State Brewing is home to a 1954 Probat coffee roaster. A 150-year-old company out of Emmerich, Germany, Probat is the leading name in coffee roasters. This particular roaster was recently discovered under a tarp in a barn in France. It was sent back to Germany for a meticulous refurbishment that took two years. It was also enhanced with some modern controls. Heiges purchased this contraption to beautifully roast fifty pounds of beans at a time. It is proudly displayed in the Copper State taproom.

From the very first day, Copper State Brewing has lived out its mission statement: "Connecting people. Creating experiences. Crafting great beer." The team wanted it to be a place where people gathered. They wanted to build a community surrounded by well-crafted beer. Walk into the taproom at almost any time of day, and you'll see they've accomplished this and are continuing to make the experience even better.

Over two years in, Jon and crew strive to grow, adapt and experiment. While continuing to brew the regular favorites and rotate seasonal beers, Jon enjoys the three-barrel pilot system. This provides Jon the freedom to push his creativity when coming up with new beer recipes in hopes of finding everyone's next favorite. This could be the now well-known Coffee Peanut Butter Porter on Nitro or any number of the sour beers Jon loves to play around with.

Last Call:

CHEERS TO GREEN BAY BEER

Beer is a social drink. Its stories are no different. Thanks for joining me as we explored over 150 years of Green Bay beer history and stories. It is my hope that the next time you drink a beer—and every pint after—you slow down, wonder about the history behind that particular beer and recognize that each brewery pours its own unique story in every glass.

There are many ways to dissect that story in a glass. You can go the technical route, analyzing the smell, mouth feel, clarity and color and tasting notes of the beer. You can look into which strain of hops is used. You can just casually approach the beer and, at the very least, find out what city it was brewed in and the name of the brewery. Talk to your beertender about the brewery. If neither of you know much about it, look up the story online or pick up a brewery book. These stories are meant to be shared. Once you know more about the story behind the beer, you'll appreciate what you're drinking even more.

As mentioned in the preface, Thrillist named Green Bay an "untapped beer city poised to blow up." Green Bay still holds spots on nationwide beer consumption leaderboards. The history of brewing in Green Bay goes back a long way. The homebrew scene is becoming more prominent. Green Bay, by all accounts, is a beer lover's paradise.

The outlook on beer and brewing in Green Bay is a positive one. The current breweries are holding strong, growing and continuing to produce high-quality, creative beer. The brewmasters work hard to provide the people of Green Bay their local beer. Even more local breweries are on the horizon.

If you want your city's beer to continue thriving and growing, do your part and continue patronizing these places.

Beer tourism is part of travel now. Visiting cities to experience local breweries brings people all over the country. Invite your out-of-town friends to Green Bay to show off our breweries. Go visit those friends in their respective cities and ask for the rundown on their local breweries. You'll notice some similarities—each brewer is passionate about his or her product and story. You'll notice some differences—every beer is as unique as the person behind it.

Disclaimer: Please enjoy your beer responsibly and never drink and drive.

Cheers to Green Bay beer—past, present and future.

BIBLIOGRAPHY

"Agriculture to Tavern Culture Exhibit." Neville Public Museum.

American Home Brewers Association. https://www.homebrewersassociation. org.

Baltimore Deutsche Correspondent. March 7, 1876.

Blesch, Francis. Will dated 1879. Brown County Probate, Green Bay, WI.

Brewers Association: For Small & Independent Craft Brewers. https://www. brewersassociation.org.

Buckley, Frank. *Enforcement of the Prohibition Laws: Official Records of the National Commission on Law Observances and Enforcement: A Prohibition Survey of the State of Wisconsin*. Washington, D.C.: U.S. Government Printing Office, 1929.

"Cicerone Certification Levels." Cicerone Certification Program. https:// www.cicerone.org/us-en/cicerone-certification-levels.

Cole, Harry Ellsworth. *Stagecoach and Tavern Tales of the Old Northwest*. Carbondale: Southern Illinois University Press, 1930.

"Constitution, Bylaws, and Policies of the Green Bay Rackers Homebrewing Club." December 1998. https://www.rackers.org/constitution-bylaws-and-policies.

Daily State Gazette. August 4, 1870.

———. August 6, 1873.

———. August 23, 1873.

———. November 17, 1873.

———. June 24, 1874.

———. March 1, 1876.

———. April 29, 1876.

———. May 16, 1876.

———. August 22, 1876.

———. September 9, 1876.

———. December 20, 1876.

———. December 21, 1876.

———. January 4, 1877.

———. November 10, 1879.

———. January 30, 1880.

———. February 3, 1880.

———. October 16, 1880.

———. January 10, 1881.

———. January 11, 1881.

———. May 20, 1881.

———. February 27, 1882.

———. May 22, 1885.

———. March 22, 1886.

———. June 7, 1886.

———. November 5, 1886.

———. November 6, 1886.

———. June 1, 1887.

———. June 21, 1887.

———. August 5, 1887.

———. December 9, 1887.

———. July 9, 1888.

———. January 5, 1889.

Fabry, Andrew (president and founder, Badger State Brewing Company). In discussion with the author. June 25, 2019.

Falish, Alex (cofounder and head of brewing operations, Noble Roots Brewing Company) and Marv Falish (cofounder and head of sales and taproom operations, Noble Roots Brewing Company). In discussion with the author. June 17, 2019.

Foley, Betsy. *Green Bay: Gateway to the Great Waterway*. Woodland Hills, CA: Windsor Publications, 1983.

Foley, Betsy, Jack Rudolph and Harold Elder. *The Green Bay Area in History and Legend*. Green Bay, WI: Brown County Historical Society, 2004.

Green Bay Advocate. March 1, 1877.

———. October 4, 1877.

———. February 14, 1878.

———. February 21, 1878.

———. February 28, 1878.

———. September 26, 1878.

———. October 10, 1878.

———. June 19, 1879.

———. July 17, 1879.

———. April 1, 1880.

———. July 22, 1880.

———. January 13, 1881.

Green Bay Gazette. August 17, 1867.

———. August 1, 1868.

———. February 27, 1869.

———. June 5, 1869.

———. September 11, 1869.

———. April 16, 1870.

———. August 4, 1897.

Green Bay Press Gazette. June 17, 1925.

———. July 18, 1925.

———. August 7, 1925.

———. November 24, 1925.

———. December 17, 1925.

———. February 9, 1926.

———. June 10, 1926.

———. November 18, 1949.

———. July 16, 1966.

———. November 20, 1969.

———. April 29, 1979.

———. November 7, 1982.

———. August 26, 2000.

———. February 27, 2008.

———. June 2, 2016.

Green Bay Rackers Homebrew Club. https://www.rackers.org.

"Green Bay, Wisconsin—A Brief History." Wisconsin Historical Society. 2009. https://www.wisconsinhistory.org/Records/Article/CS2400.

Heil, Meredith. "10 Untapped Beer Cities Poised to Blow Up." Thrillist. February 22, 2016. https://www.thrillist.com/drink/nation/the-next-big-beer-cities-craft-beer-cities.

"Hymn to Ninkasi." Translated by Miguel Civil. From "The Hymn to Ninkasi, Goddess of Beer." Written by Joshua J. Mark. *Ancient History Encyclopedia*. March 1, 2011.

Ives, Gail. *Green Bay's West Side: The Fort Howard Neighborhood.* Charleston, SC: Arcadia Publishing, 2003.

Manitowoc Herald. March 31, 1855.

Martens, Missy (Copper State Brewing Company). In discussion with the author. June 5, 2019.

"A Modern Railway." *Headlight* (1896).

Morgan, Michael D. *Cincinnati Beer.* Charleston, SC: The History Press, 2019.

Mosher, Randy. *Tasting Beer: An Insider's Guide to the World's Greatest Drink.* 2nd ed. North Adams, MA: Storey Publishing, 2017.

Oshkosh Northwestern. July 12, 1877.

Parsons, John (owner, House of Homebrew, and president, Green Bay Rackers Homebrew Club). In discussion with the author. November 11, 2019.

Quinzio, Jeri. *Food on the Rails: The Golden Era of Railroad Dining.* Lanham, MD: Rowman & Littlefield, 2014.

Revolinski, Kevin. *Wisconsin's Best Beer Guide.* 3rd ed. Hold, MI: Thunder Bay Press, 2015.

Rothe, Clarence A. *Historical Notes Relating to the Present Rahr Green Bay Brewing Corporation.* August 19, 1960.

Rudolph, Jack. *A Pictorial History of Green Bay.* Norfolk, VA: Donning Company Publishers, 1983.

Snider, Mike. "The Year in Beer." *USA Today.* December 18, 2018.

Stiles, C.O., Deborah B. Martin and L.J. Sturtz. *A Souvenir of Green Bay.* Milwaukee, WI: Wright & Joys, 1903.

Stillmank, Brad (owner and brewer, Stillmank Brewing Company). In discussion with the author. June 11, 2019.

State Gazette. August 13, 1870.

———. July 25, 1872.

———. October 26, 1872.

———. January 27, 1873.

———. May 22, 1873.

———. July 22, 1873.

———. June 20, 1874.

———. March 3, 1877.

———. July 7, 1877.

———. October 6, 1877.

Tressler, Bill (owner and brewer, Hinterland Brewing Company). In discussion with the author. July 1, 2019.

U.S. Federal Census, 1860. Fort Howard.

U.S. Federal Census, 1870. Fort Howard.

U.S. Federal Census, 1880. Fort Howard.

Van Ells, Mark D. *On the Road Histories: Wisconsin*. Northampton, MA: Interlink Publishing Group, 2009.

Weycker, Brent (co-owner and cofounder, Titletown Brewing Company). In discussion with the author. June 5, 2019.

Wisconsin State Journal. May 6, 1853.

———. August 21, 1856.

———. August 28, 1856.

INDEX

ABOUT THE AUTHOR

Cameron Teske grew up in Crete, Illinois. He learned his appreciation and love for beer in Milwaukee, where he graduated from Wisconsin Lutheran College. He now lives in Green Bay with his son, Brekken, and his dog, Ruba. They all enjoy exploring the Green Bay area, and Cameron enjoys hanging out at the local breweries.

Visit us at
www.historypress.com